BOOKER
MEMORIAL
STUDIES

BOOKER MEMORIAL STUDIES

Eight Essays on Victorian Literature in Memory of

JOHN MANNING BOOKER

1881-1948

EDITED BY
HILL SHINE

Chapel Hill
THE UNIVERSITY OF NORTH CAROLINA PRESS

COPYRIGHT, 1950, BY
THE UNIVERSITY OF NORTH CAROLINA PRESS

Foreword

THE FOLLOWING eight studies in Victorian literature are a memorial to Dr. John Manning Booker. They do not attempt to suggest the breadth of Dr. Booker's literary interests. Nor do they attempt to give a unified view of even the Victorian field. Rather they represent independent problems upon which the eight investigators were engaged at the time of Dr. Booker's unexpected death. These scholars from various parts of the country bring together their completed essays as evidence of esteem for one who was associated with them in a broad common purpose—the advancement of Victorian studies.

The sketch of Dr. Booker's career was prepared by close friends and colleagues on the faculty of the University of North Carolina as an expression of their personal esteem and appreciation of his many contributions to the University. This sketch was adopted by the faculty as a memorial resolution.

JOHN MANNING BOOKER

JOHN MANNING BOOKER, son of William David Booker and Julia Thruston (Manning) Booker, was born in Baltimore, Maryland, March 2nd, 1881, and died at his home, Senlac, in Chapel Hill, North Carolina, on the morning of March 12th, 1948. Professor Booker's forebears were individuals of note who expressed the sturdiness of their character and determination of purpose during the Revolutionary period of this country and again during the Civil War period. During both of these periods of crisis the names of Thruston and of Booker are to be found in positions of trust and of power both civil and military.

Background is an organic and important part of a man's significance, and especially so in this case. William David Booker, the father of the subject of this sketch, was born at Belvedere, the Booker ancestral home in southside Virginia, not far from the North Carolina line. After a period of study at Hampden-Sydney College which was followed by graduating in medicine from the University of Virginia, Dr. W. D. Booker located in Baltimore for the practice of medicine, and specialized in pediatrics. His interest in and advancement of this specialty resulted in his appointment as the first Clinical Professor of Pediatrics at the Johns Hopkins Medical School. These events took place in the early years of the Johns Hopkins University so that his son, John Manning Booker, came at first indirectly and later directly under the influence of this university of a new order for this country in learning and in the advancement of learning.

Thus the ideals of the Johns Hopkins University were to set John Booker's course and mold his academic career. From these ideals he never departed. He received the A.B. degree and several years later the M.A. degree from the Johns Hopkins University, and in 1912, after a period of study in Munich to be followed by the long stay at Heidelberg, the Ph.D. degree was awarded by the latter institution. From the commencement,

Professor Booker's graduate training was in English, especially in English philology. This order of understanding though appreciated by him for its rigorous demands as an intellectual discipline and the exactness of its scientific approach to problems of language failed to satisfy his sensitive and essentially artistic nature. He yearned for a more romantic area of thought and study in which people, their purposes and intentions as individuals and as movements of a social and economic order could be investigated in a scientific as well as a literary fashion. He found this in the Victorian Period of English literature. Here he was a master of detail as well as of the sequence of events. Through understanding gained by meticulous research he imparted to his students the thought and purposefulness of the significant economic adventures which had their origin in this period of English life. His understanding of the background for and the development of British Imperialism was profound.

The whole of Professor Booker's career as a teacher was spent at the University of North Carolina. He came to the institution in the fall of 1909 as assistant professor of English. He was raised to the full professorship in 1920. As a result of the Hopkins influence for investigation which was increased by his studies both at Munich and Heidelberg, Professor Booker was different from the usual teacher then found at this University. He was basically university-minded and not college-minded. He never departed from this concept of a university. In his teaching even of freshmen he did not indulge himself in a popular type of lecture but attempted by suggestion and the stimulation of inquisitiveness to excite the interest of his students and lead them to original sources for their information. He furnished the food for thought and conceived it to be the students' function to find the food and do the chewing. This was rigorous teaching for undergraduates in an institution of any order, and in the University of North Carolina, with its emphasis on the college, this teaching in a measure fell upon stony ground. The proof of the fineness as well as the effectiveness of this order of instruction was to be found in the fact that many of the best men in their undergraduate classes relished it and came back to him for elective courses. The right and the good have the habit of prevailing. Professor Booker in truth found himself when instructing graduate students in seminar courses. In the seminar an opportunity was afforded for the inductive method in instruction to assert itself as an effective instrument for gaining information at first hand and at a graduate level of understanding. The reports from students at such meetings were research adventures of a worthwhile order and not infrequently carried with them minor discoveries to excite an interest for further research. When a graduate student chose Professor Booker to be his director in his course of study leading to the Doctorate, the two lost themselves in this intellectual experience. The Director became father to the younger student. The relationship was intimate. No one of our knowledge had a higher regard for research endeavor than that possessed by Professor Booker, and yet, other than his dissertation, his research publications were limited. He took his place with those few noncreative scholars who spend their time and perhaps too much of their energy in acquiring information to give students and to spur them on for a creative type of scholarly life. Intellectually, Professor Booker was a giver and not a getter. His graduate students loved him and revered him.

When Professor Booker came to the University of North Carolina in 1909, many of its extracurricular activities which are now stabilized in form and in purpose were in their commencement and had not become regimented entities. This was true for interest in the drama. In this important outlet for the mind of both students and faculty Professor Booker lent his interest and energy in organizing casts for various productions, teaching the parts to the players, seeing that the costumes ran true to form and that the developed play was staged in an effective fashion. He, along with a few others of similar interest, laid the foundation for the Carolina Playmakers.

John Manning Booker

In his youth John Booker intended to be an architect. This interest never left him. During his periods abroad his spare time was spent in acquiring an understanding of the architectural development over various periods as shown by those monuments of form in Europe and the British Isles. When he came to the University of North Carolina, the old, central group of buildings were as they now are and on their fringes and at incidental points on the campus, buildings of various architectural design were erected in an indiscriminate fashion. There was no order as to design or location. At this period in the physical development of the University, Professor Booker was given a place on the newly created Faculty Buildings and Grounds Committee. At the time of his death he was the senior member of this committee. Through it he inaugurated and brought to fulfilment two extremely important measures. The first was the selection of a consulting architect of national eminence to visé all plans for structures to be erected on the University campus. The second was the acceptance, by this committee and by the University administration, of the zoning principle in the location of buildings—a principle that allows the function of a building to determine in large measure the site that building will occupy. The zoning principle as now followed was conceived, developed and mapped out through the great interest and labor of Professor Booker. Maps indicating this development were caused to be made by him and were published in *The Alumni Review* and the student-newspaper, *The Tar Heel*. The University of North Carolina will ever be indebted to Professor Booker for these two contributions.

Professor Booker was a man of convictions. One of the strongest convictions to hold him and guide him was his faith in and respect for his profession in general and for the faculty of the University of North Carolina in particular. He believed not only that such trained minds could regulate their own affairs and guide the life of students, but that the faculty should be permitted to formulate, through a central governing body

John Manning Booker

elected by its members with other committees as adjuncts and also so elected, the governing principles of the University's academic life. The report to the Administration of the faculty committee on University Government, of which Professor Booker was Chairman, embraces these concepts.

John Booker was an individual. He had his way of life and he lived it. His was a good life and worthy of infinite trust. He lived as a gentleman, in good form and with abundant consideration for the feelings and the determination of others. He was clean cut in form, in dress and in intent. No one had to surmise where he stood. He stated this for his own honest satisfaction and for the benefit of his adversary. Highly trained in his specialty as Professor of English, possessing a breadth of understanding as culture, he lived finely in his search for perfection.

Dr. Booker married Nell Lewis Battle, whose family had long been connected with the history of the University and the State of North Carolina. He is survived by her and their two daughters, Nell Battle Booker Sonnemann, an artist in New York City and wife of Dr. Ulrich Sonnemann, and Julia Thruston Booker Howard, wife of Dr. H. Lee Howard of Savannah, Georgia.

> —*George Coffin Taylor, Kenan Professor of English; Paul Woodford Wager, Professor of Rural Social Economics; and William deBerniere MacNider, Chairman, Kenan Research Professor of Pharmacology, The University of North Carolina.*

Contents

John Manning Booker
WILLIAM DEBERNIERE MACNIDER
Page vii

I

Carlyle's Early Writings and Herder's *Ideen:* The Concept of History
HILL SHINE, MACMURRAY COLLEGE
Page 3

II

Tennyson's *Locksley Hall* and Thomas Carlyle
WILLIAM DARBY TEMPLEMAN, THE UNIVERSITY OF SOUTHERN CALIFORNIA
Page 34

III

Dickens and the *Daily News:* The Origin of the Idea
GERALD GILES GRUBB, WAKE FOREST COLLEGE
Page 60

IV

Arnold's Marguerite
PAULL FRANKLIN BAUM, DUKE UNIVERSITY
Page 78

V

Carlyle and T. H. Huxley

WILLIAM IRVINE, STANFORD UNIVERSITY

Page 104

VI

The Revolt from "Rationalism" in the Seventies and Some of Its Literary Consequences

JEROME HAMILTON BUCKLEY, THE UNIVERSITY OF WISCONSIN

Page 122

VII

The Tragedy in Little Hintock: New Light on Thomas Hardy's Novel, *The Woodlanders*

CARL J. WEBER, COLBY COLLEGE

Page 133

VIII

Science in the Dramas of Henry Arthur Jones

JAMES OSLER BAILEY, THE UNIVERSITY OF NORTH CAROLINA

Page 154

BOOKER MEMORIAL STUDIES

I
Carlyle's Early Writings and Herder's Ideen
The Concept of History

THOUGH SOME ATTENTION has been given to the relation between Herder and Carlyle, more should be said on that subject.¹ In order to bring to bear the pertinent materials, the present study is divided into two parts. The first part will examine the circumstances under which Carlyle came to know

¹ Two books published in the thirties arrived at opposite conclusions with respect to Herder's influence. In *Carlyle and German Thought: 1819-1834* (New Haven, 1934), Professor Charles Frederick Harrold was primarily interested in Carlyle up to the writing of his first history. In *Carlyle and the Art of History* (Philadelphia, 1939), Mrs. Louise Merwin Young was chiefly interested in Carlyle the historian. Both scholars were of course aware that Carlyle had read Herder's *Ideen;* and both quoted from Carlyle's comment (in his journal for Dec. 3-6, 1826) after he had read the book. The earlier scholar, Professor Harrold, believed that though Herder repudiated materialism, sought a revelation of God in history, and attempted to outline a *plan* of history, he did not unequivocally state a spiritual point of view; and that therefore "Carlyle's admiration for Herder's work is so heavily qualified" (p. 157). And Professor Harrold concluded: "Herder's *Ideen* . . . repelled Carlyle by its deterministic philosophy" (p. 253). (Professor Harrold in his later edition of *Sartor Resartus* [N.Y., 1937: p. xxxviii] says that Carlyle found in Herder, among other German writers, the idea of 'Eternal Growth,' *das Werdende.*) On the other hand, Mrs. Young, apparently leaning upon secondary sources, pointed out a larger number of Herder's tenets. That is, she dealt with his views concerning nationality (*Volksgeist*, pp. 22-23), religion as the basic fabric of society (p. 47), art as revelation of Divine Idea (p. 60), "vital unity of man's psychical life" (pp. 65-66), and history as an organic evolution (as opposed to

Herder's work, and will present in chronological order his comments on Herder up to mid-1832. Then, after the grounds for the presumption of influence have been examined, the second part will consider some of the ideas—especially those that bear on historiography—that exist in common in Carlyle's early writings and in Herder's *Ideen zur Philosophie der Geschichte der Menschheit.*

I

By the time Carlyle wrote what is perhaps his most judicial comment on Herder, in 1832, he had known some of Herder's writings for a little over nine years. Those nine years include much of the formative period of Carlyle's study of German literature and thought, and they reach well into the period in which he was extending and consolidating his views to include human history, or historiography, and society. And during those years Carlyle's opinion of Herder's significance was undergoing change and development.

---

a priori systems of historical interpretation, pp. 22-26, 28, 45, 46, 67-69). In connection with that last-named point, she stressed the concept of historical periodicity and the notion that social institutions constitute the normal channel through which cyclic change takes place (pp. 45, 46, 67-69). And all along, in order to test Carlyle's relations to those Herderian tenets, she examined Carlyle's writings, and frequently quoted directly from them. Thus she gave a considerable amount of evidence for her belief that "Herder was one of the really important influences shaping Carlyle's thought" (p. 22). Still later, Professor René Wellek ("Carlyle and the Philosophy of History," (*P.Q.,* XXIII [1944]), after suggesting similarity between Carlyle's and Herder's concepts of historiography, as against the Saint-Simonian concept (pp. 58-59, 75) pointed out Herder's use of Palingenesis, of which use Carlyle certainly was aware (pp. 59-60); and commented that in Herder's writings "Carlyle could have found the conception of a dynamic evolution of alternating periods . . . , the idea of a balance or 'maximum' of every period . . . , the idea of a national physiognomy, and many more [ideas]" (p. 60). Finally, Professor Wellek added that such similarities between Carlyle and Herder could have resulted from indirect as well as from direct influence (p. 60). Thus, notwithstanding excellent suggestions made by those three scholars, the broad purposes shaping their investigations prevented their concentration upon this particular subject. As a result, we do not yet have an adequate study of the relation between Carlyle and Herder.

He seems to have come upon Herder under favorable auspices. For example, the estimable Scottish philosopher Dugald Stewart, the brilliant French interpreter Madame de Staël, and the great German poet Goethe recommended Herder.[2] But not until the spring of 1823 did Carlyle himself mention the new German writer: "Herder I have some good hopes of."[3] At the same time, he translated a page from Herder's *Zerstreute Blätter,* which, though it reminded him of Hervey, seemed to have *"something very sweet in it."*[4] He alluded further, though vaguely, to two of Herder's prize essays—on the origin of speech and on the decay of taste—and he believed that Madame de Staël had borrowed something from the latter.[5] And finally, in the same notebook entry, March, 1823, Carlyle showed his first acquaintance with Herder's *Ideen* by translating slightly over a page (from Bk. V, Ch. vi) on the subject of immortality of the soul.[6]

For the next three years he does not seem to have prosecuted very fully the new interest in Herder. Failure to do so is not surprising. He was chiefly engrossed in writing his *Life of Schiller,* in working through *Meisters Lehrjahre,* in making translations from various other writers for his *German Romance,* and in winning Jane Welsh for his wife. But his interest in Herder, though perhaps incidental during that time, did undergo some development. For example, in March, 1823, in his notes for *The Life of Schiller,* he recorded as an event Schiller's hav-

[2] In June 1818, Carlyle was reading Stewart's *Dissertation* for the second time (*Early Letters of Thomas Carlyle* [ed. by C. E. Norton: London, Macmillan and Co., 1886] I, 159-60; and Harrold's *Carlyle and German Thought,* pp. 33-37, especially p. 36). In September, 1817, he was reading Madame de Staël's *De l'Allemagne* (*Early Letters of Thomas Carlyle,* I, 119). Each of the three Parts of *De l'Allemagne* mentions Herder; Part II contains a short chapter (Ch. XXX) on Herder; and that Herder-chapter points out Herder's *Ideen* as one of the most fascinating of German productions. In March 1823, Carlyle was reading Goethe's *Dichtung und Wahrheit,* of which Pt. II, Bk. 10 contains Goethe's account of Herder at Strasburg (*Two Note Books of Thomas Carlyle* [N.Y., Grolier Club, 1898], p. 32).
[3] *Two Note Books,* p. 33.
[4] *Ibid.,* pp. 33-34 corrected by Wellek, *PQ,* XXIII (1944), 59-60, and note.
[5] *Two Note Books,* p. 34.
[6] *Ibid.,* pp. 35-36; Wellek in *PQ,* XXIII (1944), 59-60, and note.

Carlyle and Herder's Ideen

ing seen Herder at Weimar.[7] Slightly later he made a note, perhaps not intended as altogether complimentary, about Herder's hostile attitude toward Kantian philosophy (because, Carlyle said, its implications scandalized religious orthodoxy) and about Herder's favorable attitude towards Gall's "scull-doctrine" (because, Carlyle said, it was based on Herder's own *Ideen*).[8] About a year later the printed *Life of Schiller* (in *The London Magazine*) gave a very similar statement concerning Herder's relations to Kantian metaphysics and Gall's physiognomical system.[9] And for the later statement he cited as his source of information: "*Herder's Leben,* by his Widow."[10] Obviously by this time he had gone somewhat further than the excerpts of 1823, in his knowledge of Herder. And by July, 1826, in the biographical sketch of Richter, for *German Romance,* he had found in Jean Paul, who was to exert a great fascination upon Carlyle, a fourth important sponsor for Herder. ". . . Herder, from whom Richter learned much, both morally and intellectually, . . . he seems to have loved and revered beyond any other." However, said Carlyle, Herder belonged "in character, if scarcely in date, to an older school" than Richter.[11] It is worth observing that Herder here occupied only part of one footnote. Carlyle had as yet seen only a little of his significance.

In the last month of the same year, 1826, occurred what seems to have been his first extensive reading of Herder's *Ideen*. His notebook entry runs as follows:

---

[7] *Two Note Books,* p. 36.
[8] *Ibid.,* pp. 45-46: between March 6-28, 1823.
[9] *The London Magazine,* X (July 1824), 20-21, and footnote; this Part III of *Schiller* had been finished early in February, 1824.
[10] *Ibid.,* X, 20-21, footnote. With respect to Herder and Kant, see Maria Carolina Herder's *Erinnerungen aus dem Leben Johann Gottfrieds von Herder* (Herausgegeben durch Johan Georg Müller. Stuttgart und Tübingen, in J. G. Cotta' schen Buchhandlung, 1830), III, 122-31, 141-56, 196; and with respect to Herder and Gall, see III, 109, 195. There was of course an earlier edition, in 1820, but I have seen only the 1830 edition.
[11] *German Romance* (Centenary Edition: London, Chapman and Hall, 1898), II, 126, note.

What shall I say of Herder's *Ideen zur Philosophie der Geschichte der Menschheit?* An extraordinary Book, yet one which by no means wholly pleaseth me. If Herder were not known as a devout man and clerk, his book would be reckoned atheistical. Everything is the effect of circumstances and organisation: *Er war was er seyn konnte!*[12] The breath of life is but a higher intensation of Light and Electricity! This is surely very dubious, to say no worse of it. Theories of this and kindred sorts deform his whole work here and there.[13]—Immortality not *shewn* us, but left us to be hoped for, and believed by Faith.[14] Yet this world, as he thinks, sufficiently explainable without reference to another: *Humanität* the great object of Nature in all her arrangements of society; from the Troglodytes to the wits of Paris and Weimar.[15] *How* true is this? At least this ought to be *our* object. On the whole Herder shews much of it himself. If any thing he has a leaning to the *East*.[16] But indeed he loves all men and all things: his very descriptions of animals and inanimate agencies are animated, cordial, affectionate; much more so those of *men* in their varied *Thun und Treiben,* tho' perhaps the former are not less poetical.

Strange ideas about the Bible and Religion; passing strange we think them for a clergyman.[17] Must see more of Herder: he is a new species in some degree; a sort of *Browne redivivus?*—O Athens, *modern* Athens! Andrew Thomson *versus* J. Gottfried Herder; the

---

[12] The German sentence, which may be direct quotation, I have not located in Herder. However, the idea, in slightly different words, occurs frequently; sometimes it is printed in special type or otherwise singled out for stress as one of Herder's guiding principles in history (see *post*, Note 56). Though here in 1826 Carlyle disapproved of the principle, he later found it useful, as we shall see (*post*, Part II, *Concerning the Principle of Survival*).

[13] See, for example, Herder's *Ideen zur Philosophie der Geschichte der Menschheit*, Bk. II, Ch. 1. The edition now accessible to me is *Johann Gottfried Herders Werke. Answahl in acht Teilen.* Herausgegeben von Ernst Naumann. Berlin, Deutsches Verlagshaus Bong & Co., [n.d.] (Goldene Klassiker-Bibliothek). *Ideen* is included in Volumes III-VI, bound in one. Hereafter, in order to facilitate references to particular passages, I give, in addition to the Book and Chapter of *Ideen*, the Volume and Page in Naumann's edition, in parentheses.

[14] See, for example, Herder's *Ideen* IV, vi (Naumann's ed., Vol. III, p. 174); IV, vii (Naumann's ed., Vol. III, p. 174).

[15] See, for example, Herder's *Ideen*, IV, vi (Naumann's ed., Vol. III, pp. 166, 171, 172, 173); *Ideen*, V, v (Naumann's ed., Vol. III, p. 193); *Ideen*, XV, i Naumann's ed., Vol. V, p. 171).

[16] See, for example, *Ideen*, XI, iv (Vol. V, pp. 24-30).

[17] See, for example, *Ideen*, X, i-vii, especially Ch. v (Vol. IV, p. 166).

"Apocryphal Controversy" *versus* the Philosophy of Man! Certainly we are the most intellectual people in nature at present.[18]

The passage just quoted—important as it is—does not exhaust the significance that Carlyle derived from this reading of *Ideen*. One illustration of that fact is the 2½-page list of book-titles which he drew from that work, intending to use them later. And some of the works he certainly did follow-up and use.[19]

The entry just quoted deserves careful consideration in a context of Carlyle's intellectual development. Obviously here at the end of 1826 Carlyle's impressions from *Ideen* were mixed. He was wary of the early parts of the work—a wariness understandable in a man who had dropped natural religion, even Paley, in despair and had given up natural philosophy, even Newton, for the sake of humane studies. Notable too is this former theological student's feeling of suspicion toward a cleric who rationalized the inspired scriptures. But more significant, in the light of future developments of his thought, is the young man's comment, "Must see more of Herder." By Carlyle's Scottish standards, the learned German was, truly to a striking degree, a new species. And the contrast with the old is suggested by Carlyle's final words: "O Athens, *modern* Athens [i.e., Edinburgh]! Andrew Thomson *versus* J. Gottfried Herder; the 'Apocryphal Controversy' *versus* the Philosophy of Man!" Carlyle, though still cautious, was seeing differently from the very young man who, about 1817, had moved into religious scepticism.

There are good reasons for the change in viewpoint on Carlyle's part during the time since he had left off his training for the ministry. During the last seven years (1820-26) he had attained—chiefly in connection with German writers—brilliant insights into ethics and morals, an introduction to transcendental

[18] *Two Note Books*, pp. 72-73.
[19] *Ibid.*, pp. 75-77. Sixty-odd authors were included in that list. One of Carlyle's comments suggests pleased surprise to find a clergyman paying unqualified praise to Gibbon's *Decline and Fall*. Some of the other authors in the list—especially those dealing with the Middle Ages—he later used in connection with the unpublished *History of German Literature*.

aesthetics, some glimpses of a philosophic distinction between *Verstand* and *Vernunft*, a growing belief in the relativity of Time and Space, and some notion of continuity in change. Those gains—extremely significant for him as an individual—still, in 1826 and after, had to be drawn together and articulated into their broader significance. That is, Carlyle, in 1826 and for some years thereafter, was in quest of an understandable and adequate and credible exposition of a universe of moral order, to give meaning to a universe of physical change: a romantic interpretation of universal history, including and harmonizing God, Nature, and Man. In 1826, the romantic Carlyle for whom the 18th-century English deistic universe had lost its meaning—as it had even earlier lost it for Southey and Shelley—had made an important step by reading Herder's *Ideen* carefully and thoughtfully. Herder's book is still, to a 20th-century reader, a landmark for its amplitude of knowledge, its depth of insight, its integrity of interpretation, and its beauty, vividness, and clarity of presentation. It was a religious, philosophic, historical, and poetic book, all in one. And Carlyle might have looked a long time without finding a better study for him in 1826. Though parts of the book seemed at first too mechanistic for Carlyle, its moral idealism, which was Herder's deepest foundation, becomes increasingly clear as the work proceeds. And Carlyle was eventually to explore into that moral idealism and to value it highly.

Though Carlyle never carried out his later intention of writing an account of Herder and his significance in German literature, a good dozen more references to Herder do appear in various connections as Carlyle went forward in his rôle of interpreter of German literature to British readers. Three essays written in 1827 contain allusions to Herder—two of them with comments. Carlyle's first essay in *The Edinburgh Review* quoted Richter's statement that Herder was "a Priest of Nature, a mild Bramin."[20]

[20] Carlyle's *Critical and Miscellaneous Essays* (Centenary Edition: London, 1899), I, 16. This essay, "Richter," was finished by June 26, 1827.

"The State of German Literature" listed Herder with the choicest of German writers, Schiller and Goethe, in respect to literary style;[21] and with Kant, Schiller, Goethe, and Richter in respect to aesthetic theory.[22] And a long passage in the same essay listed him with the choicest English as well as the choicest German writers—that is, with the Elizabethans, as well as with Tieck, Richter, Schiller, and Goethe—in respect to a number of virtues. The virtues there stressed were poetic spirit, serenity of soul, calm harmonious strength, majestic meekness, smiling earnestness, and love and faith and humanity of nature. Those German writers, said Carlyle, fuse something of the nobleness of an older era with the science, the precision, and the scepticism of the new times. For them, Poetry dwells in Reality; and in their works, the 19th century, which stands before us in all its contradiction and perplexity, is no longer mean or barren. Those men have penetrated into the mystery of nature; for them, Art has at last yielded her secret; and in their works, the Spirit of the Age looks forth full of meaning. They are wise and good and clear men; they are believers; and their faith is the doctrine they have to teach us.[23] Obviously in that long passage Carlyle had worked considerably further into the significance of the new species of thinker; for he now, correctly, found Herder a deep penetrater into the mystery of nature and a beautiful and devout interpreter of the insight gained thereby. The final essay of 1827, the one on Zacharias Werner, shows still other findings.[24] In that essay he pointed to a crux in which he himself had struggled for over a decade. It was basically the old question of the *relative* and the *absolute* in religion. Carlyle's words were as follows:

It is a common theory among the Germans, that every Creed, every Form of worship, is a *form* merely; the mortal and ever-changing

[21] *Ibid.*, I, 50: By Oct. 19, 1827.
[22] *Ibid.*, I, 53.
[23] *Ibid.*, I, 63-66.
[24] In that essay, Carlyle first used the notable Phoenix-figure. Reasons will be indicated later (see *post*, Note 52) for believing that the Phoenix-figure in Carlyle's later work owes more of its philosophic content to Herder than to Werner.

body, in which the immortal and unchanging *spirit* of Religion is, with more or less completeness, expressed to the material eye, and made manifest and influential among the doings of men.[25]

And for examples of his point he listed Johannes Müller the historian, Schelling the philosopher, and Herder the clergyman, as holders of that theory. *Singular,* Carlyle still called the theory at the end of 1827. Yet for all of its singularity then, it was to become very familiar to the mind of Diogenes Teufelsdröckh, in the as yet undreamed-of Volume on Clothes.

During the next two years, 1828 and 1829, Herder was mentioned in only three writings. In the first place, a letter to Eckermann mentioned Herder as a reminder of a glory that was passing even in Germany, not to return. Where—Carlyle asked the young associate of old Goethe—where are the new leaders of German thought and art, to replace the dead generation of Schillers, Herders, Wielands, Kants, Fichtes, and Richters?[26] That disquieting question, with its implications of answer, was to recur later, after Carlyle had seized the thoughts that he could use from the Germans and was turning increasingly toward the practical spectacle of political change in France and of social and economic change in Britain. The second allusion to Herder, brief too, was in the essay on Novalis: ". . . here and there, in his [Novalis's] more elaborate passages, especially in his *Hymns to the Night,* he has reminded us of Herder."[27] That slight comparison of Herder and Novalis, at a time when the latter was exerting strong influence on Carlyle, recalls the earlier lists in which Carlyle had ranked Herder with other great names in Germany. The final comments on Herder during 1829 were made in Carlyle's second essay on Richter.[28] Two pas-

[25] *Essays*, I, 143: by Nov. 25, 1827. Cf. Herder's *Ideen*, I, iv (Vol. III, p. 69).
[26] "New Letters of Carlyle to Eckermann" (ed. by William A. Speck, New Haven, 1926), p. 4: Dec. 9, 1828. These letters also appeared in *Yale Review*, XV (July 1926).
[27] *Essays*, II, 44: January 1829.
[28] The summer of 1829, when Carlyle was much occupied with Luther, seems a probable date for Carlyle's acquaintance with a fifth work by Herder: Herder's edition of Luther's *Katechismus.* That book is merely recorded in *Carlyle's House*

sages show the high significance that the aging Herder had for at least one younger member of the Weimar circle. That is, Carlyle pointed out Richter's loving discipleship and spiritual sonship to Herder; he gave Richter's high estimate of Herder as a man ("If Herder was not a Poet, . . . he was something more,— a Poem!"); he quoted Richter's interpretation of Herder's art ("where Greek life-freshness and Hindoo life-weariness are wonderfully blended"); and he stated his own belief that Richter's critical sentence on Herder was "strikingly descriptive and exact."[29]

The unfinished and unpublished *History of German Literature*, upon which in its various phases Carlyle spent parts of three years, late 1829 to early 1831, shows at first glance little connection with Herder. One reason for the slight attention to Herder is obvious: the part that was actually written out extended only up to Luther. The only mention of Herder is therefore incidental. Like the passage already noted in "The State of German Literature" it contrasts poor literary style with good; and in doing so, it suggests that Herder's can be ranked in the highest class, with Schiller's, Lessing's, and Goethe's.[30] But that one bit is not the only exhibit from those years. When in August, 1830, the plan of publishing the *History of German Literature* as a whole fell through, Carlyle outlined in a letter another possibility for ultimately utilizing the materials he had gathered. He suggested holding intact the already finished part of the *History* (after making over some of it into review articles for immediate sale); producing, to follow that introductory part, certain additional essays ("one or two more, for example [on] Luther, Lessing, Herder"); articulating those parts with a main body made up of the various essays that he had already pub-

---

Catalogue (7th edition; London [after 1925], p. 100): Luther, Martin. *Katechismus, mit Erklärung von J. G. Herder* (Weimar, n.d.).
[29] *Essays*, II, 138 and 148: by the end of October, 1829.
[30] Carlyle's *History of German Literature* (MS at Yale University Library), p. 34: May 1830.

lished on contemporary German literature; rounding off the whole with a survey essay by way of synthesis and conclusion; and finally publishing, at some future time, the total collection as a *Zur Geschichte*.[31] As already pointed out, Carlyle never did produce the essay that he here in August, 1830, briefly suggested on Herder. However, the salvaging part of the suggested plan was carried out: he converted some of his historical materials into immediately marketable review articles. One such was his essay on William Taylor's *Historic Survey of German Poetry*, the publication of which by Taylor had had something to do with the failure of Carlyle's publishing plans. The searching essay on Taylor's book showed, among other things, Carlyle's dissatisfaction with Taylor's treatment of certain aspects of Herder—and especially with Taylor's scanty allusion to Herder's *Ideen*.[32] Obviously Herder's *Ideen* had by this time come, in Carlyle's mind, to occupy a place of historical importance.

Though that was the end of his specific allusions to Herder in connection with the unfinished *History of German Literature*, a deeper and broader relation between the work and Herder's concept of history can at least be suggested here. Carlyle's activities in this task of producing a literary history had brought him up against the practical necessity of working out an organic historical schema that would include eras and materials reaching far back into the Middle Ages. The fact that in considerable degree he succeeded owes more to Herder than has yet been pointed out. Under additional influences, it is true, Carlyle was later to go further, in a more clearly defined schema of historical periodicity; and that periodicity was to undergird his mature social thought. But even if his book-plans in 1830 did remain unfinished and even if in later years he was to go further than Herder's concept of history would have taken him, Carlyle's fragmentary *History of German Literature* nevertheless marks a

---

[31] J. A. Froude's *Thomas Carlyle: A History of the First Forty Years of his Life.* (New York, 1882), II, 97. The letter is dated August 21, 1830.
[32] *Essays*, II, 362: by January 20, 1831.

step in his gradual shift of interest from literary criticism to history and social thought. That change is so organically consistent with the course of his intellectual development that it now seems as if it were an almost necessary part of it. Probably the abrupt and disheartening failure of the planned *History of German Literature* actually resulted in accelerating rather than hindering a change already under way.

Upon relief from the steady pressure of work with the *History of German Literature,* Carlyle turned again to look into the chaotic stream of contemporary social and economic conditions that had produced his "Signs of the Times." A new speculative influence bearing upon history, society, art, and religion reached him in the writings of the Saint-Simonians.[33] Soon after, he undertook his most ambitious creative work, Teufelsdröckh's "Thoughts on Clothes" (later published as *Sartor Resartus*), which was to contain considerable social as well as philosophic and religious thought. Meanwhile, as he felt his way in the rapidly changing era of British Reform, he took the new voices in France seriously, as well he might. In an attempt to point out to d'Eichthal a stumbling block that he had noticed in the Saint-Simonian religion, Carlyle made an incidental allusion that is to the point here. He felt that the Saint-Simonian religion was weak in its interpretation of natural-supernaturalism; or, to use his own words, it lacked adequate symbols to represent the divine. Indeed (he continued),

if our Symbol of God is henceforth to be his own *Universe,* and our gospel the acted *History of Man,* then to my view is such religion

[33] In those writings he found, among other things, a more thoroughly worked-out scheme of historical change than he had encountered elsewhere, one for which he had felt the need in his studies for the *History of German Literature.* For discussion, see my *Carlyle and the Saint-Simonians: The Concept of Historical Periodicity* (Baltimore, 1941). Although Professor Wellek (*PQ,* XXIII [1944], especially pp. 57-59) disagrees with the thesis of that study and brilliantly attacks it, I retain my belief in its basic validity. Recalling the fact that the Saint-Simonians themselves had utilized Herder among other German thinkers, I suggest that Carlyle's use of Herder did not preclude or hinder his use of the Saint-Simonians, but indeed rather helped prepare his eclectic mind for what they could contribute.

ill-named the Saint-Simonian; inasmuch as it has been the Religion of all thinkers (tho' in far-scattered Communion), for the last half century: Of Goethe, for example; in a less distinct sort, of Schiller, of Lessing, Jacobi, Herder.[34]

That passing allusion to Herder in the spring of 1831 was the last specific mention for over a year. Indeed, it is the last but one in this study. For neither *Sartor* nor "Characteristics" (both in 1831) nor the twin essays on Boswell's *Johnson* (in 1832) alluded to Herder by name. But, as we shall soon see, those works did contain similarities to Herder's thought. Such matters will be brought out in Part Two of this study.

Carlyle's long visit to London, the scene of Reform, in 1831-32; his acquaintance with a new friend John Mill; and the death of his old guide and friend Goethe in the spring of 1832—those things together mark what we may conveniently call the end of Carlyle's predominant occupation with German writings. And in the essay in which he summed up dead Goethe's great significance, Carlyle in the summer of 1832 gave his final account of Herder. It included Goethe's version (which Carlyle had known since 1823) of the early association of Goethe and Herder at Strassburg. Carlyle's own comment—though of course primarily concerned with Goethe and at times not altogether complimentary to Goethe's older associate—is significant here. Notwithstanding the caustic element in Herder's disposition and notwithstanding various fundamental differences in the two men's natures, which Carlyle noticed, Carlyle stressed the importance of Goethe's early contact with the older and then more fully developed thinker:

> With this gifted man [Herder], by five years his [Goethe's] senior, whose writings had already given him a name, and announced the much that lay in him, the open-hearted disciple [Goethe] could manifoldly communicate, learning and enduring. . . . In Herder too, as in an expressive microcosm, he might see imaged the whole wide

[34] "Carlyle's Letters to the Socialists of 1830," *The New Quarterly* (London), II (1909), 286: May 17, 1831. These letters to Gustave d'Eichthal were first printed by Eugène d'Eichthal in *Revue Historique*, LXXXII (1903).

world of German literature, of European Thought; its old workings and misworkings, its best recent tendencies and efforts; what its past and actual wasteness, perplexity, confusion ... was.[85]

Thus Carlyle, in what is perhaps his most judicial account, estimated Herder as a figure who could answer as an index and interpreter of his time and its tendencies—the man in whom the young Goethe best could see, meeting and blending, the tides of the old and the tides of the new. Indeed, that last interpretation of Herder was not altogether new for Carlyle in 1832, for he had already approximated it in 1827, in "The State of German Literature." But the last statement, though less particular in the enumeration of Herder's literary excellencies, was more explicit in its pronouncement that Herder was an index of his age in both German literature and European thought.

Part I of this study has thus shown in some detail the circumstances under which Carlyle came in contact with Herder's writings. The German writer was recommended by four authors high in Carlyle's respect. Carlyle read, and utilized some materials from, a biography of Herder. Of Herder's own writings Carlyle came to know in some degree at least four, in addition to *Ideen*. And the great work *Ideen* he read carefully, and commented on, at the end of 1826. Furthermore it has been shown—also from Carlyle's own comments, over a period of nine years—that his estimation of Herder's significance underwent important developments during the period in which Carlyle was occupied primarily with German literature (to mid-1832). His interest in Herder's writings increased with his knowledge of them (1823-26); his interpretation of Herder's significance deepened as his own thought broadened and matured (1827); he at one time entertained thoughts of writing an essay on Herder as a figure in the history of German literature (1830); he pointedly condemned the scantiness of treatment that Taylor's *Historic Survey of German Poetry* gave to Herder's *Ideen* (1831); and, at the

[85] *Essays*, II, 422-24: about July 13, 1832.

end of the period under examination, he pronounced Herder an index of his era in European thought, as well as in German literature (1832).

II

Granted then a preliminary presumption of influence, important further suggestion lies in the similarities of thought between Carlyle and Herder. Because of limitation of space, Part II will focus attention upon one broad concept, which appears to be the most inclusive, as well as the most impressive and most significant, field of similarity. That is the broad concept of history. Even so, the presentation of materials involved will not be simple. In order to bring out the many similarities between Carlyle and Herder with respect to the concept of history, Part II will be divided into four sections: *Concerning Nature as Revelation; Concerning Human History as Revelation; Concerning Progressive Change;* and *Concerning the Principle of Survival.* All four of these sections are interrelated; and by presenting the materials in this form, we may hope to show a number of similarities—some rather detailed—bearing ultimately upon that most significant broad field of thought: History.

Both men, it is true, considered religion one of man's highest possible developments.[36] But introduction of a section here on religious faiths would involve needless repetition of evidence. The point essential for present purposes can be stated briefly: Carlyle and Herder both reverently believed in a beneficent Creator who acts in this world by means of natural law. And that belief is so basic and so pervasive that ample evidence of it will be found in each of the four interrelated sections, as we proceed.

In each of the four sections, the various points of similarity

---

[36] *E.g.*, Carlyle, *Essays*, I, 85-86 ("State of German Literature": by Oct. 19, 1827); II, 94 ("On History"; by April 12, 1830); *Sartor*, pp. 214-16 (by Aug. 4, 1831). Herder, *Ideen*, IV, vi (Vol. III, pp. 172, 174); IX, v (Vol. IV, p. 139).

under discussion will be digested and restated as compactly as possible. Although only a minimum amount of verbatim quotation from each writer can be presented in substantiation (and that only in footnotes), references will direct a reader to fuller details and to the contexts in the writings of the two men. Since Carlyle's writings here utilized extend over a number of years, and since, as already seen, chronology is of some significance in this study, the footnote quotations and references will include titles and dates, as well as volumes and pages.

CONCERNING NATURE AS REVELATION

For an understanding of the interrelated later sections of this study, as well as for a realization of the similarities between Carlyle and Herder in each particular section, it is desirable to work forward by as simple steps as possible. With respect to nature as revelation, four aspects will be noted. In the first place, both men thought of nature as an organic whole.[37] Second, organically unified nature is divine or, at least, is revelatory of deity.[38] Though both writers suggested that God and Nature

[37] Carlyle, *Sartor*, p. 72 (by Aug. 4, 1831), Teufelsdröckh: "Detached, separated! I say there is no such separation: nothing hitherto was ever stranded, cast aside; but all, were it only a withered leaf, works together with all; ... and lives through perpetual metamorphoses. ... all objects are as windows, through which the philosophic eye looks into Infinitude itself." See also *Essays*, II, 15 ("Novalis": January, 1829); I, 414 ("Voltaire": by March 31, 1829); *Sartor*, pp. 71, 151, 205, 246-47; *Essays*, III, 232 ("Diderot": by Oct. 15, 1832). Herder, *Ideen*, V, vi (Vol. III, p. 197): "Alles ist in der Natur verbunden; ein Zustand strebt zum andern und bereitet ihn vor. ... Diese Aussicht, die auf allen Gesetzen der Natur ruhet, gibt uns allein den Schlüssel seiner wunderbaren Erscheinung, mithin die einzige *Philosophie der Menschengeschichte.*" See also *Ideen*, I, i (Vol. III, pp. 60 and 61).

[38] Carlyle, *Sartor*, p. 258 (by Aug. 4, 1831), Teufelsdröckh: "We speak of the Volume of Nature: and truly a Volume it is,—whose Author and Writer is God ... Dost thou, does man, so much as know the Alphabet thereof? ... It is a Volume written in celestial hieroglyphs, in the true Sacred-writing; of which even Prophets are happy that they can read here a line and there a line." See also *Essays*, II, 198-99 ("Schiller": by Dec. 22, 1829); *Sartor*, pp. 53-54, 66-67, 72, 97, 151, 188, 264; *Two Note Books*, p. 238 (Jany. 13-14, 1832). Herder, *Ideen*, "Vorrede" (Vol. III, p. 55): "Gang Gottes in der Natur, die Gedanken, die der Ewige uns in der Reihe seiner Werke tätlich dargelegt hat: sie sind das heilige Buch, an dessen Charakteren ich zwar minder als ein Lehrling, aber wenigstens mit Treue und Eifer buchstabiert

are one, Herder's view seems more positive on that point; that is, he was more of a pantheist than Carlyle was. The writers agreed more frequently in stressing the notion that God uses nature as a means of revealing himself. Indeed, on that point, both called nature a sacred book.[39] Third, although both Carlyle and Herder understood that only part of this infinitely great nature can be penetrated into and known by human intellect, both men believed that nature is governed by law.[40] That is,

---

habe und buchstabieren werde." See also *Ideen,* "Vorrede" (Vol. III, p. 56); I, i (Vol. III, p. 60); XV, v (Vol. V, 198-99). For discussion of Goethe, Novalis, and Fichte as contributors to Carlyle's notion that nature is a revelation of the divine, see Harrold's *Carlyle and German Thought,* pp. 79-85.

Under the broad concept of Natural-supernaturalism (*i.e.,* the revelation of God in nature; the spiritual foundation underlying the material, and giving it meaning; the wonder-working of supernatural force acting through physical organs on natural things) one finds numerous parallels between Carlyle and Herder. See, for example, the passages which are too long to quote: Carlyle's *Sartor,* Bk. III, Ch. viii; and Herder's *Ideen,* V, ii (Vol. III, pp. 180-83), and V, iv (Vol. III, pp. 187-93). Natural-supernaturalism is exemplified also in man's dualism. The name Diogenes Teufelsdröckh in *Sartor* (God-sprung Devil's-dung) is of course a phase of the notion that man, on one side a digestive-apparatus, is also a God-like venerable mystery (*Sartor,* pp. 67, 192), a creature whose life is a combination beast-godhood (*Sartor,* p. 242). And those points in Carlyle's work may be related to Herder's comments that man is a *Spiesekanal* (*Ideen,* III, i [Vol. III, p. 105]) as well as a free immortal son of God (*Ideen,* III, iv [Vol. III, p. 162]), a self-contradictory representative of two worlds at once (*Ideen,* V, vi [Vol. III, pp. 197-98]). To both Carlyle and Herder this dualistic life is a proving-ground; and man's greatness, his moral development, lies in his acting upon the crude materials of necessity (*Sartor,* pp. 196-97: *Ideen,* V, vi [Vol. III, p. 198]).

[39] See *ante,* note 38. This notion that nature is a volume written in celestial hieroglyphs, Harrold (*Sartor,* p. 36, note) finds common in Novalis, Schelling, and Schiller.

[40] Carlyle, *Sartor,* pp. 256-58 (by Aug. 4, 1831), Teufelsdröckh: "What are the Laws of Nature? . . . To the wisest man, wide as is his vision, Nature remains of quite *infinite* depth, of quite infinite expansion; . . . The course of Nature's phases . . . is partially known to us: but who knows what deeper courses these depend on; what infinitely larger Cycle (of causes) our little Epicycle revolves on?" *Essays,* III, 40 ("Characteristics": by Dec. 17, 1831); III, 232 ("Diderot": by Oct. 15, 1832). Herder, *Ideen,* II, i (Vol. III, p. 86): "Wir bemerken diese Gesetze und Formen; ihre innern Kräfte aber kennen wir nicht, und was man in einigen allgemeinen Worten, z. B. Zusammenhang, Ausdehnung, Affinität, Schwere, dabei bezeichnet, soll uns nur mit äussern Verhältnissen bekannt machen, ohne uns dem innern Wesen im mindesten näher zu führen." See also *Ideen,* IV, vi (Vol. III, p. 172); IV, vii (Vol. III, p. 175); XIII, vii (Vol. V, p. 119); XIV, vi (Vol. V, pp. 166-67).

although final causes and purposes of nature cannot be fully ascertained by man, some aspects of its method and law (the *How*, rather than the *What* or *Why*) can be known. No doubt Carlyle's doctrine of Unconsciousness (which is at least suggested in Herder)[41] is connected with that idea. Finally, notwithstanding the tenet that the ultimate depths of nature cannot be fathomed, both men made without hesitation some general statements about the workings of nature. For example, nature works with an aim; and it produces and destroys its many so that a few may survive.[42] However, since such statements are intimately related to the historical problem (as well as to the natural problem) of survival through change, further consideration of them will be postponed until later, after our discussions of History and of Change.

CONCERNING HUMAN HISTORY AS REVELATION

Another broad subject upon which Carlyle and Herder show considerable agreement is the concept of human history as an organic revelation. First, to both men history (which is in several respects analogous to nature) constitutes in itself an or-

---

[41] Carlyle, *Essays*, III, 3 ("Characteristics": by Dec. 17, 1831): ". . . in all vital action, [Nature's] purpose and effort is, that we should be unconscious of it. . . . . . . the great is ever, in one sense or other, the vital; it is essentially the mysterious, and only the surface of it can be understood." Herder, *Ideen*, IV, vi (Vol. III, p. 172): "Nun sehen wir in den Werken der Natur eigentlich keine Ursache im innersten ein; wir kennen uns selbst nicht und wissen nicht, wie irgend etwas in uns wirket."

[42] Carlyle, *Essays*, III, 180 ("Diderot": by Oct. 15, 1832): "Worthy old Nature! She goes on producing whatever is needful in each season of her course. . . ." *Letters of Carlyle to Mill, Sterling and Browning* (New York, 1923), p. 49 (April 18, 1833): ". . . Nature is *infinitely* rich: the two *eggs* one eats at breakfast could have filled the whole world with winged creatures, and they are swallowed at one meal, and no damage done. So too with *geniuses;* a thousand can be spent apparently; if one gets to maturity we shall be content." See also *Sartor*, pp. 111, 174 (by Aug. 4, 1831); *Essays*, III, 3 ("Characteristics": by Dec. 17, 1831). Herder, *Ideen*, XV, ii (Vol. V, p. 176): "Millionen Geschöpfe gingen unter, die untergehen mussten; was sich erhalten konnte, blieb und steht jetzt Jahrtausende her in grosser harmonischer Ordnung." See also *Ideen*, V, ii (Vol. III, pp. 181-82); VIII, iii (Vol. IV, p. 91); IX, i (Vol. IV, p. 115).

ganic whole.⁴³ Indeed, a good deal that both men wrote concerning nature has a bearing upon their concepts of history as well. The second point follows logically enough: Human history (again somewhat like nature) also reveals the deity; but (as in the case of nature) the revelation is only a partial one. That is, extensive as man's knowledge of the revelation may be in a relative sense, that knowledge can never be complete or absolute. Both Carlyle and Herder stated repeatedly the viewpoint indicated in those last two sentences.⁴⁴ In Herder's statements, how-

⁴³ Carlyle, *Essays*, II, 83 ("On History": by April 12, 1830): "History ... is a looking both before and after; as, indeed, the coming Time already waits, unseen, yet definitely shaped, predetermined and inevitable, in the Time come; and only by the combination of both is the meaning of either completed." See also *Essays*, II, 59 ("Signs of the Times": by Aug. 5, 1829); II, 86-87, 88-89, 90 ("On History"); *Sartor* pp. 246-47 (by Aug. 4, 1831); III, 39 ("Characteristics": by Dec. 17, 1831); III, 176 ("On History Again": by May, 1833); Froude, *Thomas Carlyle*, II, 290 (Aug. 25-26, 1833; quoted from Emerson, *English Traits*, *Prose Works*, II, 165): *Essays*, III, 328 ("Diamond Necklace": by Dec. 17, 1833). Herder, *Ideen*, IX, i (Vol. IV, p. 111): "... so wird ... auch die Geschichte der Menschheit notwendig ein Ganzes, d.i. eine Kette der Geselligkeit und bildenden Tradition vom ersten bis zum letzten Gliede." See also *Ideen*, V, vi (Vol. III, p. 197); XIII, vii (Vol. V, pp. 119-20); XIV, vi (Vol. V, p. 164); XV, iii (Vol. V, pp. 184-85); XV, v (Vol. V, pp. 198-99). One notices, in passing, that both Carlyle and Herder use the mathematical term *Asymptote* in above-mentioned passages on the course of history: Carlyle, *Essays*, III, 176; Herder, *Ideen*, XV, iii.

⁴⁴ Carlyle, *Essays*, II, 89-90 ("On History": by April 12, 1830): "Better were it that mere earthly Historians should lower such pretensions ... and aiming only at some picture of the things acted, ... leave the inscrutable purport of them an acknowledged secret; or at most, in reverent Faith, ... pause over the mysterious vestiges of Him, ... whom History indeed reveals, but only all History, and in Eternity, will clearly reveal. ... History is a real Prophetic Manuscript, and can be fully interpreted by no man." See also *Essays*, I, 399, 414 ("Voltaire": by March 31, 1829); *Sartor*, pp. 36, 194, 203 (by Aug. 4, 1831. See p. 203, *n.*, for Harrold's comment on Schelling's and Novalis's use of *hieroglyphics); Two Note Books*, p. 211 (Oct. 22-24, 1831); *Essays*, III, 37, 42, 43 ("Characteristics"; by Dec. 17, 1831); III, 232 ("Diderot": by Oct. 15, 1832); III, 250-51 ("Cagliostro": by March 21, 1833); III, 169, 176 ("On History Again"; by May 1833); III, 329-30 ("Diamond Necklace": by Dec. 17, 1833); *Letters of Carlyle to Mill*, p. 82 (Dec. 17, 1833); *Essays* IV, 155 ("Chartism": 1839). Herder, *Ideen*, VII, i (Vol. IV, p. 42): "Der ganze Lebenslauf eines Menschen ist Verwandlung; alle seine Lebensalter sind Fabeln derselben, und so ist das ganze Geschlecht in einer fortgehenden Metamorphose. ... Und so wird die Menschengeschichte zuletzt ein Schauplatz von Verwandlungen, den nur der übersiehet, der selbst alle diese Gebilde durchhaucht und sich in ihnen allen freuet und fühlet." See also *Ideen*, "Vorrede" (Vol. III, pp. 56-57); XV, v (Vol. V, pp. 198-99). See also *ante*, note 40, for references to passages in

ever, one should notice that the analogy between nature and human history is stressed more than it is in Carlyle's. Thirdly, in Carlyle's and Herder's observations on history, the inductive study of historical facts is stressed. That stress, especially in Carlyle, requires careful examination and thorough consideration, for it is one of the important *differentiae* that mark off his conception of historiography from that of the German school to which Fichte, for example, belonged. Carlyle, like Herder, insisted not only upon rigorously ascertained and clearly understood facts on which to base the induction, but also upon insight into the complex interconnections of those facts, and of their meanings, in time and place.[45] Finally, with such a notion of the

---

which Herder says that man cannot penetrate into the inmost recesses of nature (which, like history, reveals God). For discussion of Fichte, Novalis, Richter, F. Schlegel, Goethe, and Schelling as contributors to Carlyle's notion of history as revelation, see Harrold, *Carlyle and German Thought*, pp. 164-68.

[45] Carlyle, *Essays*, II, 341-42 ("Historic Survey of German Poetry": by Jany. 20, 1831): "Thus the History of a nation's Poetry is the essence of its History, political, economic, scientific, religious. . . . the complete Historian of a national Poetry . . . will discern the grand spiritual Tendency of each period, . . . and how one epoch naturally evolved itself from the other. . . ." Carlyle, *Letters of Carlyle to Mill*, p. 57 (June 13, 1833): "A great result lies in these so intensely interesting Narratives; and *might*, had one the faculty, be drawn out of them; this were what I should call the highest kind of writing . . . I simply love all Books that offer me the Experience of any man or men, that give me any fraction of the History of men. . . ." Carlyle, *Essays*, III, 329-30 ("Diamond Necklace": by Dec. 17, 1833): "Study Reality . . . ; search out deeper and deeper *its* quite endless mystery: see it, know it; then . . . thou hast the firmest enduring basis: *that* hieroglyphic page is one thou canst read on forever, find new meaning in forever." See also *Essays*, II, 89, 94 ("On History": by April 12, 1830); III, 83 ("Boswell's Life of Johnson": by March 8, 1832); III, 296 ("Cagliostro": by March 21, 1833); III, 169 ("On History Again": by May, 1833); III, 326 ("Diamond Necklace"); *Letters of Carlyle to Mill*, p. 83 (Dec. 17, 1833); *Essays*, IV, 115 ("Varnhagen von Ense's Memoirs": 1838); IV, 155 ("Chartism": 1839); IV, 379-80 ("The Nigger Question": 1849). Herder, *Ideen*, XIII, vii (Vol. V, pp. 119-20); "Die ganze Menschengeschichte ist eine reine Naturgeschichte menschlicher Kräfte, Handlungen und Triebe nach Ort und Zeit.

So einfach dieser Grundsatz ist, so aufklärend und nützlich wird er in Behandlung der Geschichte der Völker. Jeder Geschichtforscher ist mit mir einig, dass ein nutzloses Anstaunen und Lernen derselben den Namen der Geschichte nicht verdiene; und ist dies, so muss bei jeder ihrer Erscheinungen wie bei einer Naturbegebenheit der überlegende Verstand mit seiner ganzen Schärfe wirken. Im Erzählen der Geschichte wird dieser also die grösseste Wahrheit, im Fassen

almost infinite complex of actual fact, any historian (whose facilities and faculties are at best strictly limited) would have to seek some reliable index, or condensed representation, of the multiple details. Much concerning that condensation, or selection-phase, in Carlyle's and Herder's concepts of history will be presented in detail in the last section of this study. Just now a related point will be noticed. That is, both Carlyle and Herder believed that each individual human being is an *index*, or reflector, of the whole complex of facts and tendencies in his times. Or, to re-state the point in their own words, a man is a microcosm reflecting the whole world around him.[46] To carry the point further here would lead off the present subject.[47]

---

and Beurteilen den vollständigsten Zusammenhang suchen . . ." See also *Ideen*, I, iv (Vol. III, p. 70); VIII, Introduction (Vol. IV, p. 69); XIII, vii (Vol. V, 120-21); XIV, vi (Vol. V, pp. 164-66); XV, v (Vol. V, pp. 198-99).

[46] Carlyle, *Essays*, II, 424 ("Goethe's Works": about July 13, 1832): "In Herder too, as in an expressive microcosm, he [young Goethe] might see imaged the whole wide world of German literature, of European Thought. . . ." See also *Sartor*, pp. 246-47 (by Aug. 4, 1831); *Essays*, III, 88 ("Boswell's Life of Johnson": by March 8, 1832); III, 181 ("Diderot": by Oct. 15, 1832). Herder, *Ideen*, V, vi (Vol. III, p. 201): "Der Ausdruck Leibniz,' dass die Seele ein Spiegel des Weltalls sei, enthält vielleicht eine tiefere Wahrheit, als die man aus ihm zu entwickeln pfleget. . . ." Herder's allusion here to Leibnitz's monadology is the third sentence before the passage that Carlyle translated from *Ideen* for his notebook in March 1823. See also *Ideen*, I, iii (Vol. III, p. 67): ". . . endlich nach allen die Krone der Organisation unsrer Erde, der Mensch, auftrat, *Mikrokosmus.*"

[47] But a footnote can supplement the text with an incidental association or two. a) Both Carlyle and Herder say that, of all men (or microcosms), the most active for good are the great men, the best men, the chosen men. (For example, see Carlyle *Two Note Books*, p. 185 [Feb. 7-14, 1831]; *Sartor*, p. 177 [by Aug. 4, 1831]; *Essays*, III, 86, 89-90 ["Boswell's Life of Johnson": by March 8, 1832]; II, 377, 379-80; ["Death of Goethe": by April 26, 1832]. And see Herder, *Ideen*, IX, i [Vol. IV, p. 116: "Nicht anders wirkt Gott auf der Erde als durch erwählte, grössere Menschen . . ."]) Stated thus briefly and barely that notion might seem to have a more important relation to Carlyle's hero concept than we can demonstrate. Actually many of the implications of Carlyle's hero-concept are not apparent to me in Herder. However, Mrs. Young's *Thomas Carlyle and the Art of History*, p. 23, makes an incidental statement that may have some bearing on the matter: "Fichte and his theory of heroes owed an immense debt to Herder." In Herder may lie a clue to various Carlyle passages that recall Leibnitz's monadology. Compare Herder in *Note* 46, *ante*, with this passage from Carlyle's *Essays* III, 88: Each man's soul is "a reflex and living image of God's whole Universe. . . ." There is also an additional reason for suspecting that Carlyle's knowledge of Leibnitz's

Carlyle and Herder's Ideen

CONCERNING PROGRESSIVE CHANGE

To the young Carlyle, one of the most difficult and sometimes oppressive phenomena in life was the ceaseless recurrence of change. For many 19th-century figures—Carlyle among them—the quest for a permanent in that flux developed into the problem of reconciling change with continuity, in the idea of progress. Carlyle had derived little satisfaction on the problem from his study of Dugald Stewart, who was his chief British guide in philosophic matters. But his readings in German brought him some hope. As early as the spring of 1822, a year before his first notebook entry on Herder, he recorded in the form of a question, his hopeful wrestling with the problem: "Truth *immer* WIRD *nie* IST?"[48] With the passage of years, the addition of

---

monadology came to him at second hand. That is, Leibnitz's writings do not figure prominently in the record of Carlyle's early readings. Though Carlyle does allude to Leibnitz at least nine times by 1834, the only work specified by title in the record of his readings is *Recueil de diverses pièces par Mrs Leibnitz, Clarke. Newton* (Amsterdam, 1728). (Sotheby and Co., *Catalogue of Printed Books . . . formerly the Property of Thomas Carlyle* . . . [London, 1932], Item 106).

[48] *Two Note Books*, p. 4. In "Characteristics" (by Dec. 17, 1831: *Essays*, III, 38) he assigned the Germanism to Schiller. (Possibly the thought derives from Schiller's *Über die ästhetische Erziehung des Menschen;* Letters XI and XIV discuss the opposition of *Werden* and *Sein*.) In December, 1826 (*Two Note Books*, pp. 83-84), within a few days of his main entry on Herder's *Ideen*, he was attempting to use the distinction between *Vernunft* and *Verstand* as the key to the solution. (See my *Carlyle's Fusion of Poetry, History, and Religion by 1834* [Chapel Hill, 1938], p. 11). And in the summer of 1830 (*Two Note Books*, p. 158) there is another pertinent entry on the problem: "Is not the Christian Religion, is not every truly vital interest of mankind (?) a thing that *grows?*" Of course *Sartor* (by Aug. 4, 1831) is Carlyle's fullest statement of his solution and its manifold implications. For example, *Sartor*, p. 40: ". . . not Mankind only, but all that Mankind does or beholds, is in continual growth, re-genesis and self-perfecting vitality." *Cf.* Herder's *Ideen*, IX, i [Vol. IV, p. 115]: ". . . indem wir eigentlich Menschen noch nicht SIND, sondern täglich WERDEN." Professor Harrold (*Sartor*, xxxviii) says: "In various forms, as in the doctrine of *Palingenesia* or the 'Phoenix doctrine' . . . we meet in *Sartor Resartus* the notion of 'universal becoming,' that dynamic conception of reality which was the peculiar gift bestowed on modern thought by the German mind. In Herder's theory of the movement of humanity; in Goethe's speculations on the progression of vegetable forms and of higher species; in Fichte's conception of the world as the progressive expression of the Divine Ego; above all, in Wilhelm Meister's moral development as an individual—in all these, Carlyle found the idea of 'Eternal Growth' (*das Werdende*)."

various progressive influences, the deepening of his own thought, and the broadening of his application of it in history and society (as well as in philosophy, aesthetics, and religion), Carlyle became a thorough-going progressive. He came to look upon change as a beneficent law of all things. That is, change is necessary, and cannot be stopped; it is generally progressive, and should be forwarded instead of hindered. That statement, which represents Carlyle's mature comments on the subject, is equally representative of Herder's comments.[49] Indeed, half a dozen of the Herder passages referred to in the preceding note (*Note* 49)

[49] Carlyle, *Sartor*, p. 189 (by Aug. 4, 1831) Teufelsdröckh: "In every new era, too, such Solution [concerning Origin of Evil] comes-out in different terms; and ever the Solution of the last era has become obsolete, and is found unserviceable. For it is man's nature to change his Dialect from century to century; he cannot help it though he would." Carlyle, *Essays*, III, 37-39 ("Characteristics": by Dec. 17, 1831): ". . . so much has become evident to every one, that this wondrous Mankind is advancing somewhither; that at least all human things are, have been, and forever will be, in Movement and Change. . . In some provinces, it is true, as in Experimental Science, this discovery is an old one; but in most others it belongs wholly to these latter days. How often, in former ages, by eternal Creeds, eternal Forms of Government and the like, has it been attempted . . . to chain the Future under the Past. . . . A wholly insane attempt; and for man himself, could it prosper, the frightfulest of all enchantments, a very Life-in-Death. . . . could you ever establish a Theory of the Universe that were entire, unimprovable . . . : man then were spiritually defunct. . .
"In Change, therefore, there is nothing terrible, nothing supernatural: on the contrary, it lies in the very essence of our lot and life in this world." See also Carlyle, *Essays*, II, 370 ("Historic Survey of German Poetry": by Jany. 20, 1831); II, 281-82 ("Early German Literature": by March 2, 1831); *Sartor*, pp. 47, 234-35, 236, 247; *Essays*, III, 39 ("Characteristics"); III, 236 ("Diderot": by Oct. 15, 1832). Herder, *Ideen*, XII, vi (Vol. V, pp. 74-75): "Endlich sehen wir . . . *wie hinfällig alles Menschenwerk, ja wie drückend auch die beste Einrichtung in wenigen Geschlechtern werde*. Die Pflanze blühet und blühet ab; . . . euer Tempel zerfällt, dein Orakelzelt, deine Gesetztafeln sind nicht mehr, das ewige Band der Menschen, die Sprache selbst veraltet; wie? und eine Menschenverfassung, eine politische oder Religionseinrichtung, die doch nur auf diese Stücke gebauet sein kann, sie sollte, sie wollte ewig dauern? So würden dem Flügel der Zeit Ketten angelegt und der rollende Erdball zu einer trägen Eisscholle über dem Abgrunde. . . Die Tradition ist eine an sich vortreffliche, unserm Geschlecht unentbehrliche Naturordnung; sobald sie aber sowahl in praktischen Staatsanstalten als im Unterricht alle Denkkraft fesselt, allen Fortgang der Menschenvernunft und Verbesserung nach neuen Umständen und Zeiten hindert: so ist sie das wahre Opium des Geistes sowohl für Staaten als Sekten und einzelne Menschen." See also *ante*, note 44. See also *Ideen*, I, iv (Vol. III, p. 69); IX, i (Vol. IV, pp. 116-17); XIII, iv (Vol. V, pp. 99-100); XIII, vii (Vol. V. pp. 122-23); XVI, iv (Vol. VI, p. 24).

are so much like Carlyle's that accurate English translations from them could be inserted in *Sartor* and "Characteristics" without injury to unity of meaning or, in some instances, without injury even to the figurative style.

In addition to what has been stated above about Carlyle's and Herder's general concept of progressive change, five special phases (or points) involved with that concept are so similar in the two writers—and so important—that they require brief notice here. One of the five is Carlyle's and Herder's likening outgrown institutions to ruined buildings which must be cleared away to give room for change.[50] The second, close kin to the first, is the famous clothes-figure.[51] Another is the Phoenix-figure, to represent continuity in change.[52] The fourth, which is inti-

[50] Carlyle, *Two Note Books*, p. 141 (about Aug. 5, 1829): "An Institution (a Law of any kind) may become a *deserted* edifice; the walls standing, no life going on within, but that of bats, owls and unclean creatures. It will then be pulled down if it stand interrupting any *thoroughfare:* if it do not so stand, people may leave it alone till a grove of natural wood grow round it, and no eye but that of the adventurous antiquarian may know of its existence, such a tangle of *brush* is to be struggled thro' before it can be come at and viewed." See also *Essays* II, 93 ("On History": by April 12, 1830); *Sartor*, pp. 193, 236 (by Aug. 4, 1831). See also *Two Note Books*, p. 262 (April 19-21, 1932) for a variation of the figure. Herder, *Ideen*, XV, Introductory passage before Chapter i (Vol. V, p. 168): "Vorübergehend ist also alles in der Geschichte; die Aufschrift ihres Tempels heisst: Nichtigkeit und Verwesung. Wir treten den Staub unsrer Vorfahren und wandeln auf dem eingesunknen Schutt zerstörter Menschenverfassungen und Königreiche...."
"Und wenn irgendein Staatsgebäude sich selbst überlebte, wer wünscht ihm nicht einen ruhigen Hingang? Wer fühlt nicht Schauder, wenn er im Kreise lebendig wirkender Wesen auf Totengewölbe alter Einrichtungen stösst, die den Lebendigen Licht und Wohnung rauben? Und wie bald, wenn der Nachfolger diese Katakomben hinweggräumt, werden auch seine Einrichtungen dem Nachfolger gleiche Grabgewölbe dünken und von ihm unter die Erde gesandt werden." See also, for the idea without the figure, *Ideen*, XII, ii (Vol. V, p. 47); XII, vi (Vol. V, p. 74); XIII, vii (Vol. V, p. 122).

[51] *E.g.*, Carlyle, *Sartor*, p. 47 (by Aug. 4, 1831), Teufelsdröckh: "... thus the Present is not needlessly trammelled with the Past.... Thus is the law of Progress secured; and in Clothes, as in all other external things whatsoever, no fashion will continue." Carlyle's early admiration for Swift, and the general similarity between Carlyle's clothes-figure and Swift's *Tale of a Tub*, perhaps need no comment here: see Harrold's *Sartor*, p. xxxiii. Herder, *Ideen*, I, iv (Vol. III, p. 69): "Alles ist auf der Erde Veränderung.... Wie sich die Kugel dreht, drehen sich auch auf ihr die Köpfe wie die Klimaten; Sitten und Religionen wie die Herzen und Kleider."

[52] The first occurrence of the figure in Carlyle's writings is the mere statement,

mately related to that Phoenix-figure in meaning, is the notion of *Palingenesia,* or rebirth, especially of social institutions.⁵³

in 1827, that Werner seems to be using the emblem of the Phoenix to shadow forth the history of his own personal faith. (*Essays,* I, 144 ["Werner": by Nov. 25, 1827]. As one may recall, in that essay, and on the same page, Carlyle mentioned Herder as an example of the German thinkers who regarded every religious creed as a form merely.) In that first occurrence, the lack of broad philosophic and historical implications allows doubt that Werner's Prologue to *Die Mutter der Makkabäer* is the real source of the Phoenix-figure as Carlyle later used it in connection with the idea of progress. A more adequate source would be Herder's *Ideen,* where are found the full implications that the mature Carlyle gave to the figure.

Carlyle, *Sartor,* pp. 236-37 (by Aug. 4, 1831), Teufelsdröckh: "'Society . . . is not dead: that Carcass, which you call dead Society, is but her mortal coil which she has shuffled-off, to assume a nobler; herself, through perpetual metamorphoses, in fairer and fairer development, has to live till Time also merge in Eternity. . . .

"'. . . what time the Phoenix Death-Birth itself will require, depends on unseen contingencies.'

"Thus is Teufelsdröckh content that old sick Society should be deliberately burnt . . . ; in the faith that she is a Phoenix; and that a new heavenborn young one will rise out of her ashes!" See also Carlyle, *History of German Literature,* p. 9 (Yale MS.: May 1830); *Sartor,* p. 244. See also, for the idea without the figure, *Essays,* II, 345 ("Historic Survey of German Poetry": by Jany. 20, 1831); III, 21 ("Characteristics": by Dec. 17, 1831). Herder, *Ideen,* I, iii (Vol. III, p. 68): "Sobald in einer Natur voll veränderlicher Dinge Gang sein muss, sobald muss auch Untergang sein, scheinbarer Untergang nämlich, eine Abwechselung von Gestalten und Formen. Nie aber trifft dieser das Innere der Natur, die, über allen Ruin erhaben, immer also Phönix aus ihrer Asche ersteht und mit jungen Kräften blühet." See also, for the idea without the figure, *Ideen,* II, i (Vol. III, p. 87); XIV, v (Vol. V, p. 161).

⁵³ *Palingenesia,* used first by Carlyle in *Sartor,* may have been derived from the Saint-Simonians. (See my *Carlyle and the Saint-Simonians,* pp. 37-38, 74-75. The Saint-Simonians, though familiar with Herder, seem to have derived the term from Ballanche.) However, as Professor Wellek has said (*PQ,* XXIII [1944], 59-60, and note), the term and the full idea underlying it were accessible to Carlyle in Herder's *Ideen.* Though I am not aware of the recurrence with the frequency that Professor Wellek suggested, at least one phase of the idea—the phase involved in the change from earthly life to heavenly life—does occur in Book V of *Ideen*— especially in Chapters iv and vi. For the term itself, used with respect to mere mortal social developments, see *Ideen,* IX, i (Vol. IV, p. 117): IX, iv (Vol. IV, p. 135). Though I have not attempted any count of Herder's uses, Carlyle used the term at least nine times within two years: six times in *Sartor* (pp. 217, 255, 268, 269, 270, 297: by Aug. 4, 1831), once in "Boswell's Life of Johnson" (*Essays,* III, 120: by March 8, 1832), once in *Two Note Books* (p. 266: April 28, 1832), and once in a letter (Froude's *Thomas Carlyle,* II, 276: March 29, 1833).

Carlyle, *Sartor,* p. 268: "In a word, do we at length stand safe in that far region of Poetic Creation and Palingenesia, where that Phoenix Death-Birth of Human

Last is the notion of the relativity of Time and Space, especially with respect to its bearing upon immortality of the soul.[54] Of those five points, most are figuratively expressed; and most carry the implication of progressive change.

CONCERNING THE PRINCIPLE OF SURVIVAL

As we have seen, Carlyle believed that deity found its most approximate revelation in human history. And he believed no less firmly that all earthly things were continually in the process of change—a change that, in the long run, would prove progressive. But in view of the innumerable facts that even the briefest historical period presents, a historian (who must deal with long

---

Society, and of all Human Things, appears possible, is seen to be inevitable?" Froude, *Carlyle*, II, 276: "Ruin economical is not far distant; and then in regard to ruin spiritual I should say that *it* was already triumphant among us; while in chaotic London there were blissful symptoms here and there discernible of *palingenesia*. . . . In London, amid its huge deafening hubbub of a Death-song, are to be heard tones of a Birth-song. . ." Herder, *Ideen*, IX, iv (Vol. IV, p. 135): "So beweinenswert dies Schiksal der Menschen im Leben und in der Geschichte ist, weil es beinah' keine Nation gibt, die ohne das Wunder einer völligen Palingenesie aus dem Abgrunde einer gewohnten Sklaverei je wieder aufgestanden wäre. . ."

[54] Carlyle, *Essays*, II, 25-26 ("Novalis": Jany. 1829): "Time and Space themselves [say the Kanteans] are not external but internal entities: they have no outward existence, there is no Time and Space *out* of the mind; they are mere *forms* of man's spiritual being, *laws* under which his thinking nature is constituted to act.

"If Time and Space have no absolute existence, no existence out of our minds, it removes a stumbling-block from the very threshold of our Theology." Carlyle, *Two Note Books*, p. 222 (Nov. 2-4, 1831): ". . . our conception of Immortality (as Dreck too has it) depends on that of *Time*. . . . Believe that there properly *is* no Space and no Time, how many contradictions become reconciled!" See also *Sartor*, pp. 55, 255, 260-62 (by Aug. 4, 1831). Harrold (*Carlyle and German Thought*, pp. 87-95) discusses the inadequacy of Carlyle's understanding of Kant on Time and Space, especially on the *formal* nature of Time and Space. Herder, *Ideen*, V, vi (Vol. III, p. 202): "Schon in ihren [the Soul's] gegenwärtigen Fesseln sind ihr *Raum* und *Zeit* leere Worte; sie messen und bezeichnen Verhältnisse des Körpers, nicht aber ihres innern Vermögens, das uber Raum und Zeit hinaus ist, wenn es in seiner vollen innigen Freude wirket. Um Ort und Stunde deines künftigen Daseins gib dir also keine Mühe . . ." The passage just quoted from Herder may take on additional significance in view of the fact that it occurs in Book V, which deals with immortality of the soul; and in view of the fact that the passage leads immediately into the *Ideen*-passage that Carlyle translated in his notebook in March, 1823.

periods, in which the revelation is forever changing form) requires some working principle of compression, or selection, in order to evaluate and interpret the materials with which he deals. The principle of selection, or rather of survival, upon which Carlyle finally settled was essentially a moral one.[55] With respect to the possible derivation of that principle of survival, the first step for our attention is Carlyle's and Herder's belief that *all things become and do what they can become and can do*.[56] The second step is the belief, held by both men, that moral power is the basis of all other power: in Carlyle the commonest terms used to describe that moral power were *moral, true, good,* and *worthy;* in Herder, the commonest terms were *truth, goodness, justice (Billigkeit)* and *reason (Vernunft)*.[57] Putting to-

[55] The fact that Carlyle was for a while confused between two systems of morality, which for the sake of brevity may here be distinguished as the *Romantic* and the *Puritanic*, need not enter largely into the present discussion. See my *Carlyle's Fusion of Poetry, History, and Religion*,—especially Part III.

[56] Carlyle, *Essays*, I, 19 ("Richter": by June 26, 1827): ". . . the great law of culture is: Let each become all that he was created capable of being. . . . There is no uniform of excellence, either in physical or spiritual Nature: all *genuine* things are what they ought to be." See also *Sartor*, p. 40 (by Aug. 4, 1831); *Essays*, III, 36-37 ("Characteristics": by Dec. 17, 1831); *Letters of Carlyle to Mill*, p. 85 (Dec. 17, 1833); *Essays*, IV, 164 ("Chartism": 1839). Herder, *Ideen*, XII, vi (Vol. V, p. 70): "Was ist das Hauptgesetz, das wir bei allen grossen Erscheinungen der Geschichte bemerkten? Mich dünkt dieses: *dass allenthalben auf unserer Erde werde, was auf ihr werden kenn. . .*" See also *Ideen*, XIII, vii (Vol. V, p. 119): XIV, vi (Vol. V, p. 167); XV, i (Vol. V, p. 174); XV, ii (Vol. V, p. 176); XV, v (Vol. V, pp. 202, 202-3). In the passage last referred to, Herder says: "Mit diesem Leitfaden durchwandre ich das Labyrinth der Geschichte und sehe allenthalben harmonische göttliche Ordnung; denn was irgend geschehen kann, geschieht; was wirken kann, wirket. Vernunft aber und Billigkeit allein dauren; da Unsinn und Torheit sich und die Erde verwüsten."

[57] Carlyle, *Essays*, III, 38 ("Characteristics": by Dec. 17, 1831): "The True Past departs not, nothing that was worthy in the Past departs; no Truth or Goodness realized by man ever dies, or can die; but is all still here, and, recognised or not, lives and works through endless changes." See also *Essays*, I, 399-400 ("Voltaire": by March 31, 1829); II, 73, 75, 78 ("Signs of the Times": by Aug. 5, 1829); *History of German Literature*, pp. 13, 20 (Yale MS.: May 1830); *Two Note Books*, p. 171 (Sept. 9, 1830); *Essays*, II, 278-79 ("Early German Literature": by March 2, 1831); *Sartor*, p. 225 (by Aug. 4, 1831); *Essays* III, 76, 100 ("Boswell's Life of Johnson": by March 8, 1832); II, 378 ("Death of Goethe": by Apr. 26, 1832); *Two Note Books*, p. 265 (April 22-28, 1832); *Essays*, III, 160, 166 ("Corn-Law Rhymes": about May 4, 1832); III, 171-74 ("On History Again": by May 1833); IV, 116 ("Varnhagen von Ense's Memoirs": 1838); *On Heroes, Hero-Worship, and the Heroic in History*

gether those two steps, one can now state Carlyle's and Herder's principle of survival (or compression, or selection) in history, as follows. Out of the welter of individual thoughts, actions, facts, and institutions of the past, the morally worthiest and greatest survive, by virtue of that worth: and thus they are the ones that bear fruit in later times. To the historian, that survival, which is itself the proof of essential worth, furnishes the criterion by which to select and compress and interpret past facts, and by which to prognosticate future developments along the earlier-established lines of tendency.[58] Finally, notwithstanding that principle of orderly survival, accidents have happened, and will continue to happen. Both men took that fact into consideration in several passages. That is, to man's way of reasoning, the course of history has frequently seemed to turn upon accidents, ec-

---

(London, 1898), pp. 61-63 (1841); *Essays*, IV, 305 ("Dr Francia": 1843). Herder, *Ideen*, XV, iii (Vol. V, p. 184-85): *"Drittes Naturgesetz. Ebensowohl ist's erwiesen, dass, wenn ein Wesen oder ein System derselben aus diesem Beharrungszustande seiner Wahrheit, Güte und Schönheit verrückt worden, es sich demselben durch innere Kraft, entweder in Schwingungen oder in einer Asymptote wieder nähere, weil ausser diesem Zustande es keinen Bestand findet."* See also last quotation in note 56, *ante*. See also *Ideen*, XII, ii (Vol. V, p. 47); XV, iii (Vol. V, p. 184, 188, 191); XV, iv (Vol. V, pp. 196, 198); XV, v (Vol. V, 202).

[58] A very important thing to remember is Carlyle's well-founded and frequently repeated insistence that power is basically moral, or spiritual, rather than physical. (See, in addition to references included in Notes 56 and 57, *ante*, the following: *Essays*, II, 92 ["On History": by April 12, 1830]: *Letters of Carlyle to Mill*, p. 34 [Jany. 12, 1833; when taken with Froude's *Carlyle*, II, 263, note]; *Essays*, IV, 123, 146, 147, 148, 176 ["Chartism": 1839]; IV, 372- 73 ["The Nigger Question": 1849].) Notwithstanding the clarity of his general view on that point, he has been frequently misunderstood. Though he was himself occasionally frankly confused when considering contemporary phenomena in social history, especially of the 19th Century, he did not retreat from his principle of survival of the morally worthiest. A sentence or so may suggest the explanation. That is, in certain vortex-eras in the world's history (as, for example, the 19th century), old moral boundaries were confused or sometimes obliterated; and new and perhaps deeper aspects of right, which were only fitfully glimpsed at first, had to be experimentally worked out toward their full significance. Naturally enough in those vortex-eras, the conduct of Chosen Men, the seers who had the deepest moral insight and therefore the greatest power, was frequently at odds with conventional morality. Although in such eras, Rights and Mights could at first appear "frightfully discrepant" (*Essays*, IV, 147 ["Chartism": 1839]), in the long run the two prove equal—or rather proportionate, as cause and result.

centricities, or trivialities; but for both Carlyle and Herder, such accidents tend, in the long run, to correct each other and to fit into a scheme of order.[59] Thus, to both Carlyle and Herder, a basically moral principle of survival interpreted the law of change as progress, and interpreted no less the notions of history and nature as revelation.

A brief recapitulation will emphasize the main points of evidence presented in Part II of this study. After noting generally the religious stamp of both men's minds, Part II has discussed in some detail four concepts that both Carlyle and Herder held in common. All four relate to the broad concept of history. In the first place, nature, an organic unity, is revelatory of divinity. But of that infinitely great nature, mankind can know only a relatively small part: at most, something of the law that governs it. Second, human history, which is somewhat analogous to nature, also constitutes an organic whole. It, like nature, reveals God. But that revelation also is incomplete, and absolute knowledge is again impossible for man. Nevertheless, through intelligent study of actualities and their complex interrelations, much

[59] Carlyle, *Sartor*, pp. 49-50 (by Aug. 4, 1831), Teufelsdröckh: "By what strange chances do we live in History? Erostratus by a torch; Milo by a bullock; . . . Boileau Despréaux (according to Helvetius) by the peck of a turkey . . ." *Essays*, III, 173-74 ("On History Again": by May 1833): "In fact, here [in history] as elsewhere, what we call Accident governs much; in any case, History must come together not as it should, but as it can and will.

". . . Thus does Accident correct Accident; and in the wondrous boundless jostle of things (an aimful POWER presiding over it, say rather, dwelling *in* it), a result comes out that may be put-up with." See also *Essays*, III, 272-73 ("Cagliostro" by March 21, 1833); III, 426 ("Mirabeau": 1837). Herder, *Ideen*, XIII, vii (Vol. V, pp. 121-22): "Nun ist unsere Aufklärung unstreitig ein grosses Ding in der Weltgeschichte . . . Und dennoch von welchen kleinen Umständen hing sie ab, die uns das Glas und einige Bücher brachten . . ." *Ideen*, XV, v (Vol. V, p. 202): "Was irgend geschehen kann, geschieht und bringt hervor, was es seiner Natur nach hervorbringen konnte. Dies Naturgesetz hindert keine, auch nicht die ausschweifendste Macht an ihrer Wirkung; es hat aber alle Dinge in die Regel beschränkt, dass eine gegenseitige Wirkung die andre aufhebe und zuletzt nur das Erspriessliche daurend bleibe. Das Böse, das andre verderbt, muss sich entweder unter die Ordnung schmiegen oder selbst verderben." See also *Ideen*, XV, iii (Vol. V, pp. 184-85); XV, v (Vol. V, pp. 202-3).

insight into historical fact and law can be gained. Third, in both nature and human history, one of the very important principles is change. Change, which is a law of all things, is, on the whole, progressive. Fourth, since the correlative of change is continuity, both men formulated a principle of survival in history. That is, out of the welter of ceaseless change, the morally worthiest and greatest survive and produce fruit for later times. Thus the principle of survival of the morally greatest and worthiest is the criterion by which the historian can select, compress, and interpret his materials.

Though the last-named point—the moral principle of survival—has been discussed purposely in this study as one of the constituent elements in a philosophy of history, the principle itself is worthy of special notice. It is, as has been suggested, the clue which (in spite of Carlyle's early theological and philosophic confusions and in spite of his late social, economic, and political discouragements) bound his concept of progressive change into a whole with his notions of history and nature as revelations of deity. And its further implications are very extensive. Whether one regards Carlyle as a historian, a social reformer, a critic of literature, an interpreter of German transcendentalism, or a religious teacher, that principle is perhaps the one that gives his thought, in its many facets, its greatest unity of meaning.[60] As Goethe understood, early in 1828, Carlyle's deepest foundation was moral.

One is of course aware that other writers besides Herder had much to do with all the phases of thought that have been considered in this study. Nevertheless, Carlyle's interest in Herder, his study of *Ideen,* and the similarities between his early writings and *Ideen* perhaps constitute evidence of special indebtedness. Influence is not notable with respect to social thought or aesthetics, except as those fields are seen as historical vistas. The

---

[60] Though the late Professor Harrold with his usual insight gave some attention to this principle (*Carlyle and German Thought,* p. 176) he was unable to suggest specific sources for it.

influence that passed from Herder to Carlyle—modified and supplemented as it was by other influences—was at the high level where religion, philosophy, and history merge into one. And the evidence is clearly traceable in the years when Carlyle was formulating his philosophy of history—a philosophy that reconciled and articulated together as a whole, and at the same time as a process, Nature, God, and Man.

HILL SHINE

MacMurray College

II

Tennyson's Locksley Hall *and* Thomas Carlyle

"MOST OF THE LIVING WRITERS of our time bear some trace of Carlyle in their works," wrote John Wilson in 1881, "even those who are in other respects unlike him. Do we not, for instance, find the poet-laureate giving forth this purely Carlylean utterance, as if the spirit of the Chelsea sage, struggling to find for itself expression in polished verse, had taken temporary possession of Tennyson?"[1] He proceeded to quote a seven-line passage from *Maud*. But when Churton Collins wrote in 1891 a bookful of passages from authors whom Tennyson paralleled, echoed, or imitated—or may have so treated—he made no mention of Carlyle.[2] On his title-page Collins printed a quotation from the laureate to show that Tennyson himself considered it desirable for a poet to avail himself of the works of others:

> And well his words become him; is he not
> A full-cell'd honeycomb of eloquence
> Stor'd from all flowers?
> Tennyson: *Edwin Morris*

It has long been recognized that Tennyson, though not a plagiarist, derived ideas for his poetry frequently from the works

[1] Rev. John Wilson, *Thomas Carlyle: The Iconoclast of Modern Shams. A Short Study of His Life and Writings* (Paisley, 1881), pp. 101-02.
[2] John Churton Collins, *Illustrations of Tennyson* (London, 1891).

of other writers, and often admittedly. But not Collins, Lounsbury, Rolfe, Hallam Tennyson, the poet himself, Starnes, Darch,[3] or anyone else, so far as I know, in the very long list of students of Tennyson, has ever suggested that Tennyson made use of *Sartor Resartus* in writing *Locksley Hall;* nor has any student of Carlyle.

This article has as its purpose (1) to increase the interest of at least one famous poem by Alfred Tennyson, namely *Locksley Hall*, (2) to provide new indication of Tennyson's poetic skill, and (3) to strengthen and increase our appreciation of the great influence wielded by Thomas Carlyle.

The history of the fame accorded to *Locksley Hall* for more than a century must be considered in another study, although I am tempted to present a few chronologically well-separated comments in order to indicate the high quality of the regard in which this poem has usually been held.

Critics and historians have shown surprising variations in their statements about the date when Tennyson wrote *Locksley Hall*. The poem first appeared in print in 1842. How much earlier had it been composed? Roberts and Bushnell state that

---

[3] Collins, *op. cit.*, also his edition of Tennyson's *Early Poems* (London, 1900); Thomas R. Lounsbury, *The Life and Times of Tennyson* (New Haven, 1915); W. J. Rolfe (ed.), *The Poetic and Dramatic Works of Alfred Lord Tennyson* (Cambridge edition, Boston and New York, 1898); Hallam Tennyson, *Alfred, Lord Tennyson; a Memoir by His Son* (London, 1897, hereinafter referred to as *Memoir;* Hallam Tennyson (ed.), Tennyson's *Works*, annotated by Alfred, Lord Tennyson, the Eversley edition; *Poems* (London, 1908), hereinafter referred to as "Eversley ed., *Poems*"; D. T. Starnes, "The Influence of Carlyle upon Tennyson," *Texas Review*, VI (1921), 316-36; Alice Maddeford Darch, *A Comparison of Tennyson's* In Memoriam *and Carlyle's* Sartor Resartus (unpublished master's thesis, University of Western Ontario, London, Ontario, Canada, 1927). For the others in the list I cite here only Archibald MacMechan (ed.), *Select Poems of Alfred Tennyson* (Boston and London, 1907); and I cite this because of the previous excellent study MacMechan had made of *Sartor—cf.* Archibald MacMechan (ed.), *Carlyle: Sartor Resartus*, in the Athenæum Press Series (Boston and London, 1896). Hereinafter his edition of *Sartor* is referred to as "MacMechan."

About Tennyson's use of other authors we have his own statement preserved: ". . . as far as I know, nothing of mine after the date of 'Timbuctoo' was imitative. As for being original, nothing can be said which has not been said in some form or another before" (*Memoir*, I, 45-46n.).

it was "probably written in the early 1830's."[4] Tennyson himself declared that in 1830 he "went by the first train from Liverpool to Manchester," and that "at that time"[5] he composed the line "Let the great world spin for ever down the ringing grooves of change." Chew says "the date of composition is uncertain, though at least one line . . . is as early as 1830."[6] Turnbull lists it as written in 1835.[7] The DeVane edition states that it "bears evidence of having been written at High Beech, Epping Forest, Tennyson's home after 1837."[8] Luce supposes it to have been written "a few years before 1842."[9] Lounsbury says unqualifiedly: "We have no means of ascertaining when it was written, still less when it was conceived."[10] The poet's son, in 1908, says merely that it was first published in 1842, giving no mention of date of composition.[11]

Not many sources have been suggested for the poem as a whole. Through the years there has been a persistent attempt to read autobiography into the story, but Tennyson denied that his own life served as source, and others also have declared the recurrent contention to be untenable.[12]

We have Tennyson's own statement about the provenience

[4] John H. Roberts and Nelson S. Bushnell, *Outline Guide to Major English Poems (1660-1890)*. . . . (New York, 1938), p. 154. Harold Nicolson sets the date of composition as "in the early 'thirties"—see his *Tennyson: Aspects* . . . (London, 1923), p. 252.

[5] *Memoir*, I, 195; Eversley ed., *Poems*, II, 344. In the first edition, however, the line reads "Let the peoples spin. . . ."

[6] Samuel C. Chew (ed.), *Tennyson: Representative Poems* (New York, 1941), p. 191.

[7] Arthur Turnbull, *Life and Writings of Alfred Tennyson* (London and New York, 1914), p. 214.

[8] William Clyde DeVane and Mabel Phillips DeVane (eds.), *Selections from Tennyson* (New York, 1940), p. 430.

[9] Morton Luce, *A Handbook to the Works of Alfred Lord Tennyson* (London, 1895), p. 376—the same statement appears on the same page of the revised edition (1914).

[10] T. R. Lounsbury, "The Two Locksley Halls," *Scribner's Magazine*, VI (1889), 250.

[11] Eversley ed., *Poems*, II, 340.

[12] See *Memoir*, II, 379; Eversley ed., *Poems*, II, 341; Sir Charles Gavan Duffy, *Conversations with Carlyle* (London, 1892), p. 5; Henry J. Jennings, *Lord Tennyson. A Biographical Sketch* (London, 1884), pp. 84-85.

of the poem—"an imaginary place and imaginary hero"—and his son noted in his journal in 1890 that according to his father the poem was "a simple invention as to place, incidents and people."[13] These blunt remarks have in all probability caused numerous persons who might otherwise have been source-seekers to think that the author was indebted to no written, printed, or spoken account by another, and to no personal experience of his own, as a basis for *Locksley Hall*—even as a partial basis. But the statement may actually mean that the author took his reading of various sorts and his other experiences of various sorts, worked them together in his own mind, and finally expressed them by his own enriching language, so that he felt justified in declaring the poem to be entirely the product of his own imagination. It may also imply that the characters he presented in his retelling had never existed in real life, were originally the product, so far as he knew, of someone else's imagination.[14]

There is sufficient support for the interpretation expressed in the last two sentences above. Certainly Tennyson is reported as saying that Sir William Jones' prose translation of the Arabic *Moâllakât,* hanging up in the temple of Mecca, "gave him the idea of the poem."[15] Moreover, he indicated to his son that from the prose account of African travel by Pringle, which he had been reading in 1837, he took the figure of the hungry lion approaching at night the people around a slowly dying fire.[16] Also he said that the line using the figure of the new steam railway train was written on the basis of a personal experience, as I have

---

[13] Eversley ed., *Poems,* II, 340; *Memoir,* II, 379.

[14] He may indeed have heard Carlyle himself refer to *Sartor Resartus* as being entirely imaginary: "symbolical myth all" (see MacMechan, p. xxiii).

[15] *Memoir,* I, 195; II, 491. It has already been pointed out that a very little of the poem is in any way derived from the Arabic story; see W. D. Paden, *Tennyson in Egypt. . . .* (Lawrence, Kansas, 1942), p. 32; also W. D. Paden, "Tennyson and Persian Poetry, Again," *Modern Language Notes,* LVIII (1943), 655; and earlier, John Churton Collins (ed.), *The Early Poems of . . . Tennyson* (New York and London, 1900), p. 198; E. G., "Tennyson and the Mo 'Allakàt," *Spectator,* XCII (1904), 290.

[16] *Memoir,* I, 162; Eversley ed., *Poems,* II, 343.

shown above.[17] Also, at least one part, the allusion to Joshua's moon in Ajalon, is based on the Bible. Then his son implies that the poet drew from personal experience his vivid picture of "the light of London flaring like a dreary dawn."[18] FitzGerald indicates that this poem describes "Lincolnshire coast: about Mablethorpe, where A. T. stayed much,"[19] and Walters is even more emphatic about this.[20] Several publications have pointed out in *Locksley Hall* parallels and echoes (if not conscious borrowings) of passages in other works, especially the classics.[21] To be sure, Tennyson at times showed great irritation concerning persons who had found parallels and had indicated that he had borrowed, or even plagiarized.[22] Nevertheless, he admitted that poets do take suggestions from books and recognized his pleasure and the pleasure of other readers in the "peculiar charm" of passages in poetry where the authors have adopted the creation of previous poets and proceeded "to reclothe it, more or less, according to their own fancy";[23] and it is well known that he often made use of stories that he had read or heard, not only in the *Idylls* and his plays and other long poems—*Enoch Arden*, for instance—but also in short compositions, as the two Northern Farmer poems, *The Charge of the Light Brigade,* and many others.[24] In the second volume of the 1842 *Poems,* wherein

---

[17] In addition to *Memoir,* I, 195, see Alfred Gatty, "A Line in 'Locksley Hall,'" *Notes and Queries,* 8th ser., II (1892), 387; and especially John Cuming Walters, *In Tennyson Land.* . . . (London, 1890), p. 48.
[18] *Memoir,* I, 150; see also Eversley ed., *Poems,* II, 342-43.
[19] *Ibid.,* II, 342; see also *Memoir,* I, 192n.
[20] Walters, *op. cit.,* p. 22.
[21] See works by Collins and by Luce, cited above; W. P. Mustard, *Classical Echoes in Tennyson* (New York, 1904); J. Cuming Walters, *Tennyson: Poet, Philosopher, Idealist* (London, 1893), pp. 33off.; Edna T. Moore, *Tennyson's Use of the Bible* (Göttingen and Baltimore, 1917).
[22] Jennings, *op. cit.,* pp. 257-62; Willingham Franklin Rawnsley, "Recollections of Tennyson," *Nineteenth Century,* XCVII (1925), 195; *Memoir,* I, 256; Evan Charteris, *The Life and Letters of Sir Edmund Gosse* (New York and London, 1931), pp. 194-95.
[23] Jennings, *op. cit.,* p. 261.
[24] Baum speaks of Tennyson's "usual search for subjects"; see Paull F. Baum, *Tennyson Sixty Years After* (Chapel Hill, 1948), p. 319.

Locksley Hall first apeared, he added, as a final note, that stories by Miss Mitford and Miss Ferrier had "partly suggested" his *Dora* and *Lady Clare*.

Tennyson has, indeed, a long-standing reputation as a poetic adapter of the stories and the ideas of other people. We may recall here, as an indication, the comment by Walters that "Tennyson never invented a plot,"[25] and the statement in the *Memoir* to the effect that he was sometimes impressed by a phrase and kept turning it over and over in his mind until finally he produced his own version, variation, or elaboration of it.[26]

What story available to Tennyson before 1842 was able to provide a suggestion from which *Locksley Hall* might have grown? It is the story told by Thomas Carlyle in Book II of *Sartor Resartus*, the account of the unhappy love affair of Diogenes Teufelsdröckh. This had appeared first in the pages of *Fraser's Magazine* in 1833-34, and later as a book in Boston, Massachusetts, in 1836, and in London, in 1838. Carlyle's letters and journal reveal to us the difficulty he had in getting *Sartor* into *Fraser's*, and the definite unpopularity of its initial appearance.[27] Froude made this impressively clear; but he also showed that *Sartor* was read and highly praised by a few people of the sort whom Tennyson would be likely to know and respect. The fact of importance at this point in our study is that *Sartor* was available to Tennyson at any time from 1834 on, and would be called to his attention before 1842 in such ways that he could scarcely avoid reading it, however hastily. James Spedding, Leigh Hunt, John Sterling, and W. M. Thackeray each could have served to bring Tennyson and Carlyle together, and together in so intimate a manner that Tennyson would have felt forced to

---

[25] Walters, *Tennyson:* . . . , p. 329.
[26] *Memoir*, I, 268.
[27] James Anthony Froude, *Thomas Carlyle. A History of the First Forty Years* . . . *1795-1835* (New York, 1882), II, 33, 62, 67, 71, 74. Froude couples the names of Carlyle and Tennyson during the 1840's, in his *Thomas Carlyle* . . . *1834-1881* (New York, 1884), I, 50.

know something of Carlyle's *Sartor*. I mention only four;[28] there were a larger and an increasing number of men in the years 1834-1841 who could have brought together these two literary men, both of whom were in process of growing in social prestige as well as in literary productivity and fame.

Henry J. Jennings, author of a careful biographical account in 1884 of Tennyson, in dealing with the years 1837-42 points out that "very little has been chronicled about his movements during this period" and proceeds to give what information he can. Included is the following:

> During this period he formed the acquaintance of Thomas Carlyle, and the two great spirits found much in common. A friendship based upon a close accord of tastes sprang up between them. They went for long walks together, far into the night; they often dined together at the Cock tavern in the Strand; they met at Carlyle's house in Chelsea, and had 'wit combats,' recalling those of Shakespeare and Ben Jonson at the Mermaid. An auditor of some of those discussions speaks of the richness of fancy, the fulness of philosophic thought, the grand roll of argument which characterized them. . . . Carlyle, there can be little doubt, had a considerable influence upon Tennyson.[29]

In the introduction to his edition of *Sartor* in 1896, MacMechan stated flatly that during the nine silent, sad years between 1833 and 1842 Tennyson was Carlyle's friend, and that the two "seem to have had numberless unchronicled smokes and talks together." These years are the time when Tennyson was improving his art and was, MacMechan reminds us, thinking out the problems of *In Memoriam*. He points out some "verbal resemblances" between that poem and *Sartor,* and announces that

---

[28] See *Memoir*, I, 150, 156, 163-64, 181; Gordon Ray (ed.), *The Letters of William Makepeace Thackeray* (Harvard University Press, 1945-46), I, 347, 413, II, 56ff.; Emery Neff, *Carlyle* (New York, 1932), pp. 143, 216; Frances M. Brookfield, *The Cambridge "Apostles"* (New York, 1907), pp. 274-75, *et passim*.

[29] Jennings, *op. cit.*, pp. 80-81. He repeats this in his revised and enlarged edition (London, 1892), pp. 48-49. See also William Macneile Dixon, *A Tennyson Primer* . . . (New York, 1896), p. 10.

there is good reason to believe that "Carlyle's Sartorian philosophy" helped Tennyson deal with the perplexities suggested by Hallam's death.[30]

Tennyson's son asserts that his father did not become intimate with Carlyle until after 1842;[31] he is influenced in this assertion by a statement, which he quotes, made by FitzGerald. But FitzGerald harbors a mistaken impression. We need only to look elsewhere in the *Memoir* to find a letter from Carlyle dated September 5, 1840, which shows that Tennyson at that time was far beyond the stage of mere acquaintanceship with Carlyle.[32] Froude prints, apparently from Carlyle's journal entry made in July, 1840, a passage that appears also in the letter of September 5th in the *Memoir;* and Froude indicates that in July Carlyle "admired and almost loved Tennyson."[33] In several books, furthermore, there appears record that surely as early as 1838 both Carlyle and Tennyson were original members of that carefully chosen group of men who met for dinner together in London once a month to discuss literature and the world in general—a group known first as the Anonymous Club, and soon as the Sterling Club, in honor of their founder, the brilliant son of the publisher of the London *Times*.[34]

During March, 1839, the minor authoress Louisa Lanesborough spent some time in the home of the Tennysons. Her journal pictures a very pleasant home life, with Alfred jolly

---

[30] MacMechan, p. lxx; for influence of *Sartor* on *In Memoriam* see also Thomas Bayne, "Carlyle and Lord Tennyson," *Notes and Queries*, 7th ser., XI (1891), 204; also Darch, *op. cit.*, and Starnes, *op. cit.*

[31] *Memoir*, I, 188. Hallam shows his uncertainty about FitzGerald's testimony by omitting the earlier part where FitzGerald says that he does not think that Carlyle was even acquainted with A. T. until after the appearance of the 1842 volumes; and by speaking of intimacy rather than acquaintance. *Cf.* the Eversley ed., *Poems*, II, 337.

[32] *Memoir*, I, 187n. See also *ibid.*, I, 181, for Sterling's letter dated Oct. 26, 1841; note also Emily Tennyson's comments, *ibid.*, I, 214.

[33] Froude, *Thomas Carlyle . . . 1834-1881, op. cit.*, I, 33.

[34] As secretary, Spedding listed the members—see Brookfield, *op. cit.*, pp. 301-03; Thomas Carlyle, *The Life of John Sterling* (New York, Vol. XI of the Centenary ed. of Carlyle's *Works*), p. 159.

socially, and interested in literature, including German. It is clear that he often went to London for the day and evening.[35]

At this time I need go no farther into the question of the contacts between Tennyson and Carlyle: it is sufficient to have shown that the poet knew Carlyle well and in all probability was acquainted with *Sartor Resartus*, by 1841 at the latest. And the question of why he might have desired to keep quiet about his poetic indebtedness to Carlyle may be left to another article.

"The Teufelsdröckhian dialect," wrote Frederic Harrison,[36] "is obscure even to its select students." And we learn elsewhere that John Stuart Mill, certainly no mental weakling, announced his getting very little from *Sartor* as he read it for the first time; and that John Sterling also reported reading it twice.[37] What a reader finds truly worthwhile after such difficult reading he will feel proud of having learned, will wish to pass on to others. Tennyson's supposed reading of *Sartor* before 1842 may well have caused him to decide that the message of Teufelsdröckh's love story should be made known to many, and yet have caused him to realize that the story must be "translated" into more attractive form before many would read it.

The poem *Locksley Hall* is his translation, it seems to me, of *Sartor Resartus*, Book II. The materials already presented in this paper and the parallels that will now be pointed out give what I consider sufficient support to this contention.

The action of the poem is very slight: a young man sends his comrades on ahead, while he looks at the beautiful country estate called Locksley Hall, where he has loved and because of his relative poverty has been rejected at the insistence of the girl's

---

[35] Bartle Teeling (ed.), "A Visit to the Tennysons in 1839," *Blackwood's Magazine*, CLV (1894), 605-21.

[36] Frederic Harrison, *Studies in Early Victorian Literature* (London and New York, 1895), p. 67.

[37] *Autobiography of John Stuart Mill. Published for the First Time without Alterations or Omissions* . . . (Columbia University Press, 1924), p. 123; Carlyle, *Life of Sterling, op. cit.*, p. 108.

(Amy's) parents, who have caused her to marry a dull and coarse but wealthy country landowner; he broods bitterly and resentfully over the weakness of Amy and the unfairness of the social system; he tempts himself to give up his vision of helping mankind locally and internationally by the tools of intellect and the new science; he then determines to go forward, to live and work in accord with his vision; he sets out to rejoin his comrades.

Sartor Resartus is a combination of the reform essay and the didactic novel. As MacMechan says, it is "a novel—with appendixes, fore and aft."[38] Of the three books that compose *Sartor,* Book II is the novel proper, the biography of Diogenes Teufelsdröckh which Carlyle himself declares to be "a symbolic Adumbration, significant to those who can decipher it." The main outlines of the love story in it were taken over from his unfinished novel, *Wotton Reinfred.*[39] Although, as MacMechan wrote, "it is hard to connect Teufelsdröckh the sage with Teufelsdröckh the perfervid lover and desperate skeptic," the passion is very realistic and the love affair the very heart of the book, successfully arousing the reader's sympathy for the sufferings of Teufelsdröckh.[40] Within Book II Carlyle includes this story: the indigent young German visionary meets at a country estate the lovely Blumine; they fall in love; he is rejected by order of her family; he sets off on wanderings, learns that she has married a dull but wealthy country squire; he suffers "a hot fever of anarchy and misery raving within," broods bitterly, becomes irreligious, is dominated by the Everlasting No; he protests against this domination, but he wonders whether he will ever be more than a Nobody (the Centre of Indifference); he achieves a renunciation of desire for Happiness, which is selfish, and gains a desire for Blessedness, which can come only from unselfish concern for and activity for the welfare of all mankind; he is convinced of the active presence of God (the Ever-

---

[38] MacMechan, p. xli.
[39] See *ibid.,* pp. 411, xxii, xxiii-xxiv.
[40] *Ibid.,* pp. xl; xxix; also, for the originals of Blumine, see p. xxxv.

lasting Yea) everywhere, tending toward a Universal Association of the sound portion of mankind; finally, he goes forward actively, in a life of letters, among all people, especially the intellectual, and declares: "With or without perceptible result, I am minded diligently to persevere."

"Thus have we," Carlyle concludes, "as closely and perhaps satisfactorily as, in such circumstances, might be, followed Teufelsdröckh through the various successive states and stages of Growth, Entanglement, Unbelief, and almost Reprobation, into a certain clearer state of what he himself seems to consider as Conversion."[41]

The parallel between the two stories is strikingly close. Without any further evidence one would be inclined to say that Tennyson has extracted the symbolical heart of *Sartor Resartus*, compressed its action, and turned it into poetry predominantly lyrical yet retaining the original dramatic tension between the Everlasting No and the Everlasting Yea.[42]

Other parallels—in characterization and description, in narrative details, in words and phrases—are numerous, so numerous indeed that all cannot be cited here. I shall proceed, however, to set forth a good many of them, enough to indicate that there is indeed ground for belief that Tennyson built his poem upon Carlyle's prose.

First, the young man, the speaker and central character in Tennyson's story, is strikingly similar, indeed almost identical, in all characteristics to the central character in Carlyle's.

Tennyson's speaker reveals himself to be a young man intellectually curious, with "an angry fancy" his only equipment for making a material success in life. He is apparently a poet, and one who depends largely upon "ancient founts of inspiration" for whatever he will write concerning the world of his time, with its new physical and political science. He blusters, and he

[41] *Sartor Resartus*, Bk. II, Chap. X.
[42] The setting provided by Tennyson is English, authentic Lincolnshire—as shown earlier in this study; see Notes 19, 20.

declares " 'Tis well that I should bluster"; he thinks he may be mad; he fears he may spend the rest of his life living over again in sadness and deep gloom his disappointing experience; he has a palsied heart and a jaundiced eye to which all earthly things seem disordered, out of joint; his foolish passion sweeping through him has left him dry; he is ashamed to have been so upset; but he is upset, even though he knows his words are wild; finally, however, he steadies himself, he regains by intellectual insistence a sense of purpose in a life amid modern progress; and though he will not strive to be happy, in physical self-indulgence, he will seek to be noble—to grow, to work with all his talents, to aid in the progress of the world.

In *Sartor Resartus*, Diogenes Teufelsdröckh is a young man with a little figure, with patience of research, philosophic and even poetic vigor, and unhappily with prolixity and tortuosity and manifold ineptitude[43] (pp. 13, 24).[44] Many a deep glance, and often with unspeakable precision, has he cast into mysterious Nature, and the still more mysterious Life of Man (pp. 25-26). He is wonder-loving and wonder-seeking, striking with force of vision and of heart into the mystery of the World; and he can not recommend, finally, a return to the savage state (p. 188). He speaks of his atrabiliar moods, and Carlyle reminds us that all men are to a certain extent hypochondriac (p. 54). In Book II of *Sartor*, Teufelsdröckh recollects his childhood in rose-colored light, as poets are wont to do (p. 81). Then he presents himself as a young man with an excess both of love and of fear, with keen ardor of feelings (p. 118), with ideas that he sometimes expresses ironically, a young man who, by some, may be viewed as a pest to society, who has a devilishness of temper (p. 119). He declares himself to have been, at the time of his love affair, a "Diogenes flame-clad, scaling the upper Heaven, and

---

[43] The spelling "inaptitude" appears in *Fraser's Magazine*, VIII (1833), 590.
[44] Such page references are to MacMechan, as giving a text widely available and the same in every important detail, indeed in very nearly all details, as the text in *Fraser's*.

verging towards Insanity, for prize of a 'high-souled Brunette,' as if the Earth held but one and not several of these" (p. 131); he is a young man without a profession (p. 121) and with proud timidity, wakened to a sense of self-respect and purpose in life by the love his beloved Blumine shows for him (p. 131).[45] When she tremulously announces to him that they are to meet no more, he breaks out in passionate expostulations, entreaties, indignations, but all is in vain; " 'Farewell, then, Madam!' said he, not without sternness, for his stung pride helped him" (p. 134). Carlyle comments that to the less philosophical readers "it is now clear that the so passionate Teufelsdröckh, precipitated through 'a shivered Universe' in this extraordinary way, has only one of three things which he can next do: Establish himself in Bedlam; begin writing Satanic Poetry; or blow-out[46] his brains. In the progress towards any of which consummations, do not such readers anticipate extravagance enough; breast-beating, brow-beating (against walls), lion-bellowings of blasphemy, and the like" (p. 135). Actually Diogenes is struck with a feverish vision of "green Paradise-groves in the waste Ocean-waters" (p. 136);[47] internal Unrest seems his sole guidance, and he wanders as if a curse has fallen upon him; he wanders "into the wilds of Nature; as if in her mother-bosom he would seek healing" (p. 137); the marriage of his Blumine to the dull country squire is made known to him, and as the bride and groom proceed on their way oblivious of him, his knowledge "seems to have withered-up what little remnant of a purpose may have still lurked in him" (p. 140). He wanders about confusedly, or wishes that he might wander about (p. 141, l. 18), through all quarters of the world,[48] disappointed, bemocked of Destiny; yet he feels

---

[45] This immediately calls to mind Tennyson's *Maud*. For suggestion that *Maud* echoes *Sartor* in a few specific lines, see MacMechan, p. 372.

[46] *Fraser's*, IX (March, 1834), 306, shows no hyphen between "blow" and "out."

[47] *Locksley Hall*, l. 164, reads: "Summer isles of Eden lying in dark-purple spheres of sea."

[48] He reports his having wandered, in real life or imaginatively, at one time "as Hadjee in the neighbourhood of Mecca" (p. 141). A Hadjee is simply a

always an instinctive and compelling urge to go forward: "A nameless Unrest urged me forward; ... forward must I ... still Forward! ... From the depths of my own heart, it called to me, Forwards! The winds and the streams, and all Nature sounded to me, Forwards!" (pp. 142-43).[49] He declares that at that stage he "was even, once for all, a Son of Time, a child of the Time-Spirit" (pp. 143, 117).[50] Wandering wearisomely through this world, he becomes wholly irreligious: "Doubt had darkened into Unbelief" (p. 146). He exclaims, in his wild way: "Is there no God then: but at best an absentee God, sitting idle, ever since the first Sabbath, at the outside of his Universe" (p. 147).[51] We

---

Mohammedan who has performed the Hajj or pilgrimage to Mecca. It is possible that this phrase recalled to Tennyson's mind the reading he had done some years earlier of the translation by Sir William Jones of the first poem of the *Moallakat* (this spelling is Sir William's), with the explanatory comment by Sir William (see his *Works*, 6 vols., London, 1799, IV, 243-57). Thus Carlyle's phrase may have indirectly suggested to Tennyson the setting for *Locksley Hall*, the idea for which he said was directly given him by Sir William's work—see Note 15 above, and the text to which it is appended. As a setting or framework not provided by Carlyle, Tennyson presents his Teufelsdröckh in England, like the central character in the Arabian narrative, leaving a band of comrades in order to brood in solitude at a place where formerly his beloved had loved him.

[49] *Locksley Hall*, l. 181: "Not in vain the distance beacons. Forward, forward let us range." The writing of this line may have called back to Tennyson's mind the figure, based on the railroad, that he put next, expressed in a line he later declared he had written in 1830: "Let the great world spin for ever down the ringing grooves of change." (Actually this line appeared in the first edition as "Let the peoples spin. . . .") Then, too, Carlyle had mentioned earlier (p. 36) "those Liverpool Steam-carriages," in commenting upon the progress of mankind.

A striking bit of evidence that Carlyle's conversation in the years before 1842 may have repeated powerfully his *Sartor* theme—which is clearly the theme of *Locksley Hall*—appears as the final passage in a letter dated August 28, 1841, which he wrote to two young Edinburgh men who had written him for advice: "Through many difficulties and confusions, you need not doubt a good issue, if you have strength to endure honestly, manfully. Your help lies within yourself; your hindrance too lies there. Courage. Forward, forward!" (Francis Espinasse, *Literary Recollections and Sketches*, London, 1893, p. 60.)

[50] Tennyson's character speaks, after his dreams of wild wanderings over the earth, declaring himself a child of the times: "Mother-Age . . . , help me as when life begun" (l. 185). *Cf.* also l. 108: "Hide me from my deep emotion, O thou wondrous Mother-Age!"

[51] *Cf. Locksley Hall*, l. 137: "Yet I doubt not thro' the ages one increasing purpose runs." *Cf.* also Teufelsdröckh's remark (p. 151): "To me the Universe was

might pitifully enough call our Diogenes wicked, for such wild utterances, says Carlyle, and yet, unprofitable servants as we all are, perhaps at no era of his life was he more decisively the Servant of Goodness, for he nevertheless still loved Truth, and would bate no jot of allegiance to her. " 'Truth!' I cried, 'though the Heavens crush me for following her: no Falsehood! though a whole celestial Lubberland[52] were the price of Apostasy' "[53] (p. 148). Dimly present also with Teufelsdröckh at this time is the Infinite nature of Duty, the need of knowing what thou thyself *canst work at* (p. 149). Next he is strengthened to go to meet all approaching storms of life: the temper of his misery is changed: not Fear or whining Sorrow is it, but Indignation and grim fire-eyed Defiance (p. 153). He observes that "Arcturus and Orion and Sirius and the Pleiades are still shining in their courses" (p. 165).[54] He later realizes that "these mad shadow-hunting and shadow-hunted Pilgrimings of his were but some purifying 'Temptation in the Wilderness,' before his apostolic work (such as it was) could begin" (p. 168). "Often also," says Teufelsdröckh, "could I see the black Tempest marching in anger through the Distance [p. 170] ... Always there is a black spot in our sunshine: it is even, as I said, the *Shadow of Ourselves* [p. 173] ... I asked myself: What is this that ... thou hast been

---

all void of Life, of Purpose, of Volition, even of Hostility": this expresses the negative attitude that he was to reject before long. *Cf.* also the paragraph (pp. 224-25) indicating his complete assurance of ever-continuing progress, together with emphasis upon the need for individual effort.

[52] The word *Lubberland*, a favorite repeatedly with Carlyle (see MacMechan, p. 348), means a luxurious land of tropic beauty, physical comfort, and laziness— a land of lotus-eaters. Tennyson makes the speaker in *Locksley Hall* tempt himself with the amplified and richly detailed visualization of just such a land, physically glorious but inhabited by lubbers, with narrow foreheads, beast-like, barbarian, squalid; *cf.* the section of the poem soon to be quoted.

[53] The spelling "Apostacy" is in *Fraser's*, IX (1834), 312.

[54] *Cf. Locksley Hall*, ll. 8-9, indicating the shining of Orion and the Pleiades. Tennyson's mention of these constellations has been thought to indicate indebtedness to the *Moállakát* translated by Sir William Jones—see E. Koeppel, "Tennysoniana. II. Sir William Jones's Uebersetzung der 'Moallakat' und 'Locksley,'" *Englische Studien*, XXVIII (1900), 400-06; and Paden, *Tennyson in Egypt* ..., *op. cit.*, p. 32.

fretting and fuming, and lamenting and self-tormenting, on account of? Say it in a word: is it not because thou art not HAPPY? Because the THOU (sweet gentleman) is not sufficiently honoured, nourished, soft-bedded, and lovingly cared-for? Foolish soul! [p. 174] . . . let him who gropes painfully in darkness or uncertain light . . . lay this precept well to heart . . . : *'Do the Duty which lies nearest thee,'* which thou knowest to be a Duty! Thy second Duty will already have become clearer' [p. 177] . . . Divine moment, when over the tempest-tost Soul, as once over the wild-weltering Chaos, it is spoken: Let there be light! [p. 178] . . . I too could now say to myself: Be no longer a Chaos, but a World, or even Worldkin. Produce! Produce! . . . Whatsoever thy hand findeth to do, do it with thy whole might. . . ." (p. 179).

At this point the last thirty-eight lines of Tennyson's poem will make clear many parallelisms with what has been indicated in the preceding text and accompanying notes:[55]

. . . to burst all links of habit—there to wander far away,
On from island unto island at the gateways of the day.

Larger constellations burning, mellow moons and happy skies,
Breadths of tropic shade and palms in cluster, knots of Paradise.

Never comes the trader, never floats an European flag,
Slides the bird o'er lustrous woodland, droops the trailer from
   the crag;

Droops the heavy-blossom'd bower, hangs the heavy-fruited tree—
Summer isles of Eden lying in dark-purple spheres of sea.

There methinks would be enjoyment more than in this march
   of mind,
In the steamship, in the railway, in the thoughts that shake
   mankind.

[55] They contain also some phrases and ideas that will be alluded to later in this paper.

There the passions cramp'd no longer shall have scope and
   breathing-space;
I will take some savage woman, she shall rear my dusky race.

Iron-jointed, supple-sinew'd, they shall dive, and they shall run,
Catch the wild goat by the hair, and hurl their lances in the sun;

Whistle back the parrot's call, and leap the rainbows of the brooks,
Not with blinded eyesight poring over miserable books——

Fool, again the dream, the fancy! but I *know* my words are wild,
But I count the gray barbarian lower than the Christian child.

I, to herd with narrow foreheads, vacant of our glorious gains,
Like a beast with lower pleasures, like a beast with lower pains!

Mated with a squalid savage—what to me were sun or clime?
I the heir of all the ages, in the foremost files of time—

I that rather held it better men should perish one by one,
Than that earth should stand at gaze like Joshua's moon in
   Ajalon!

Not in vain the distance beacons. Forward, forward let us range.
Let the peoples spin for ever down the ringing grooves of change.

Thro' the shadow of the world we sweep into the younger day:
Better fifty years of Europe than a cycle of Cathay.

Mother-Age (for mine I knew not) help me as when life begun:
Rift the hills, and roll the waters, flash the lightnings, weigh
   the Sun—

O, I see the crescent promise of my spirit hath not set.
Ancient founts of inspiration well thro' all my fancy yet.

Howsoever these things be, a long farewell to Locksley Hall!
Now for me the woods may wither, now for me the roof-tree fall.

Comes a vapour from the margin, blackening over heath and holt,
Cramming all the blast before it, in its breast a thunderbolt.

Let it fall on Locksley Hall, with rain or hail, or fire or snow;
For the mighty wind arises, roaring seaward, and I go.

—*Poems* (London, 1842), II, 108-11.

If we look at the character of Blumine, in *Sartor*, we find her to be a very close prototype of the young lady in Tennyson's work. Blumine is utterly lovely in the mind of the young Teufelsdröckh, yet is vaguely presented, a symbolical creature: "For, without doubt, the title *Blumine*, whereby she is here designated, and which means simply Goddess of Flowers, must be fictitious." Carlyle proceeds to refer to the young man as "the Lover" and to her as "the Loved." The name of Tennyson's heroine, Amy, now immediately suggests the translation of the concept of "the Loved" into a not uncommon English name, Amy, which is based on the French *aimée*. Flora, of course, as Carlyle indicates, would be a close translation of Blumine as goddess of flowers, but Tennyson, if he derives his heroine from Carlyle's, seems more concerned with her as an object for love. Carlyle describes Blumine with this sentence: "We seem to gather that she was young, hazel-eyed, beautiful, and some one's Cousin: highborn and of high spirits;[56] but unhappily dependent and insolvent; living, perhaps, on the not too gracious bounty of moneyed relatives" (p. 125). Tennyson's Amy is made Cousin Amy, and the parallel is striking in other details also, even to the eyes—"All the spirit deeply dawning in the dark of hazel eyes"—and Baker's *Concordance* shows that nowhere else does Tennyson provide one of his characters with hazel eyes;[57] incidentally, a few paragraphs later Carlyle speaks of "her dark eyes." Where does she live? Teufelsdröckh is rhapsodic; "Noble Mansion! There stoodest thou, in deep Mountain Amphitheatre, on umbrageous lawns, in thy serene solitude; stately, massive, all of granite; glittering in the western sunbeams, like a palace of El Dorado, overlaid with precious metal. Beautiful rose up, in wavy curvature, the slope of thy guardian hills" (p. 126); and the Gardenhouse, where Diogenes goes to attend a tea, he finds

---

[56] *Fraser's*, IX (1834), 303, has "spirit"; later in the sentence *Fraser's* has "monied" for "moneyed."

[57] Arthur E. Baker, *A Concordance to the Poetical and Dramatic Works of Alfred, Lord Tennyson*. . . . (London, 1914).

similarly glorious in its environment: ". . . in front, from the wide-opened doors, fair outlook over blossom and bush, over grove and velvet green, stretching, undulating onwards to the remote Mountain peaks: so bright, so mild, and everywhere the melody of birds and happy creatures." Here it is that his fancy lightly turns to thoughts of love, though, as he himself says of Blumine, her sphere is too far from his; how should she ever think of him? Tennyson is selective, and he adds details, notably of the seashore, appropriate to English Lincolnshire; but it is not too much to say that Carlyle could have suggested the very manor house of Locksley Hall.

In the presence of Blumine, the young Diogenes is successful in discomfiting a Philistine, a crude bore among the conversationalists. His intellectual superiority is evident to all, especially to Blumine, who smilingly admires him (p. 129). "At parting, the Blumine's hand was in his: in the balmy twilight, with the kind stars above them" (p. 130). Diogenes is increasingly smitten with love. Writing of himself, he declares that

"day after day, like his heart's sun, the blooming Blumine shone on him. . . . 'She looks on thee,' cried he; 'she the fairest, noblest; do not her dark eyes tell thee, thou art not despised? The Heaven's-Messenger! All Heaven's blessings be hers!' Thus did soft melodies flow through his heart; tones of an infinite gratitude; sweetest intimations that he also was a man, that for him also unutterable joys had been provided.

"In free speech, earnest or gay, amid lambent glances, laughter, tears, and often with the inarticulate mystic speech of Music; such was the element they lived in; in such a many-tinted, radiant Aurora, and by this fairest of Orient Light-bringers must our Friend be blandished, and the new Apocalypse of Nature unrolled to him! Fairest Blumine! And, even as a Star, all Fire and humid Softness, a very Light-ray incarnate! Was there so much as a fault, a 'caprice,' he could have dispensed with? Was she not to him in very deed a Morning-Star; did not her presence bring with it airs from Heaven? As from Æolian Harps in the breath of dawn, as from the Memnon's Statue struck by the rosy finger of Aurora, unearthly music was around him, and lapped him into untried balmy Rest" (pp. 131-32).

With this last sentence in mind we may recall here one of the most famous couplets[58] in Tennyson's poem:

> Love took up the harp of Life, and smote on all the chords with might;
> Smote the chord of Self, that, trembling, pass'd in music out of sight.

Teufelsdröckh never understood how Blumine could have found determination, even on hest of Necessity, to cut-asunder these so blissful bonds. But Carlyle calls him foolish, since he had no prospect of capital, no means of respectably supporting her, and declares, "Pshaw! thy divine Blumine, when she 'resigned herself to wed some richer,' shows more philosophy ... than thou." Having recounted the origin and the splendid growth of this Love-mania, Carlyle briefly tells of its almost instantaneous dissolution (p. 133). He uses the vivid figure of a balloon ascension and the explosion of the balloon.[59] The following passage is perhaps largely responsible for Tennyson's passage on commercial aviation and "airy navies" and the raining down of "ghastly dew":

> We view, with a lively pleasure, the gay silk Montgolfier start from the ground, and shoot upwards, cleaving the liquid deeps, till it dwindle to a luminous star: but what is there to look longer on, when once, by natural elasticity, or accident of fire, it has exploded? A hapless air-navigator, plunging, amid torn parachutes, sand-bags, and confused wreck, fast enough into the jaws of the Devil! Suffice it to know that Teufelsdröckh rose into the highest regions of the Empyrean, by a natural parabolic track, and returned thence in a quick perpendicular one.

[58] Tennyson declared that it presented one of his finest figures; see the Eversley edition, *Poems*, II, 343.

[59] Clark Emery went into great detail in considering whether Tennyson had in writing this poem a conception of the heavier-than-air type of airship; having no thought of the balloon in *Sartor*, he decided that "there is no reason save Tennyson's lack of explicitness to assume that in this passage he was thinking only of the balloon"; see his "The Background of Tennyson's 'Airy Navies,'" *Isis*, XXXV (1944), 139-47.

Briefly, in the words mostly of Diogenes, Carlyle (p. 134) suggests the final parting. One morning the young man found Blumine silent, she seemed to have been weeping; tremulously she announced they were to meet no more. After his resultant outburst,

> She put her hand in his, she looked in his face, tears started to her eyes: in wild audacity he clasped her to his bosom; their lips were joined, their two souls, like two dew-drops, rushed into one,—for the first time, and for the last.

Source hunters and compilers of parallels have long busied themselves over the hauntingly effective line in *Locksley Hall* that reads:

> And our spirits rush'd together at the touching of the lips.

No one, so far as I know, has ever found another passage that begins to approach the above sentence in *Sartor* as a probable basis for Tennyson's line.[60]

Though the ordering of details in *Locksley Hall* differs sometimes from that in *Sartor*, and Tennyson's work sometimes has more, sometimes fewer details than Carlyle's, much in the two is similar, including, as we have seen, the characters named Blumine and Amy. What of the husband of Amy? The speaker in *Locksley Hall* jealously characterizes Amy's husband as a country gentleman who is a boor, a gross clown, a hard rider after the hounds, an intemperate drinker, with a range of lower feelings, a narrower heart than his. Carlyle had shown Blumine's husband in a less jaundiced light, but he is nevertheless a not impossible foundation for Amy's husband. Blumine was married to an English country squire whom Teufelsdröckh had known

---

[60] For Carlyle's words "their two souls, like two dew-drops, rushed into one" Charles Frederick Harrold, in his edition of *Sartor Resartus* (New York, 1937), p. 145, n. 3, suggested as source or parallel the words "their two souls, like two tears, melted into one" written by Carlyle himself in translating Richter's "Life of Quintus Fixlein"; see Carlyle's *German Romance*, Centenary ed., II, 253. That Tennyson made direct use of Richter's passage or Carlyle's translation rather than of *Sartor* is highly improbable—quite apart from the fact that *Sartor* provides the important word "rushed"—and I believe that no one ever has suggested that he did so.

for some time previously. His name was Herr Towgood, or, "as it is perhaps better written, Herr Toughgut." Diogenes had become acquainted with him at the university; he was a young person of quality, from the interior parts of England, distantly related to and highly esteemed by Blumine's guardians.

Towgood had a fair talent, unspeakably ill-cultivated; with considerable humour of character: and, bating his total ignorance, for he knew nothing except Boxing and a little Grammar, showed less of that aristocratic impassivity,[61] and silent fury, than for most part belongs to Travellers of his nation. . . . Towgood was not without an eye, could he have come at any light. . . . Towards this young warmhearted, strongheaded and wrongheaded Herr Towgood, I was even near experiencing the now obsolete sentiment of Friendship. . . . I felt that, under certain conditions, I could have loved this man. (pp. 105-07)

Another detail relating to characterization is that the speaker in Tennyson's poem is an orphan, even as Teufelsdröckh. He calls the Age his mother, saying "Mine I knew not"; and refers to his father as having fallen in "wild Mahratta battle," in India. Teufelsdröckh, reared by two loving foster-parents, was bereaved of both of them (pp. 96, 113) by the time he left college; and his own parents he never knew. He had been brought as a tiny infant in a basket to his foster-parents by an imposing stranger, who left some gold coins, an insufficient number, and washed his hands of the boy for ever after. This of course could suggest Tennyson's phrase "a selfish uncle's ward." The basket was made to hint an oriental birthplace for Diogenes: it was overhung with green Persian silk, a rich veil under which the foster-parents thought might possibly be some "Pitt diamond"— the famous Pitt Diamond had been brought from India. The speaker in *Locksley Hall* refers to "yonder shining Orient, where my life began to beat," where the Mahrattas lived.

[61] Here (p. 105) as in some other places (*e. g.*, pp. 107, 224-25) is indication that Tennyson may have leaned upon Carlyle directly and indirectly when he turned, many years later, to composing *Locksley Hall Sixty Years After*.

It seems possible that Carlyle's mention of "a hungry lion" (p. 114) may have recalled to Tennyson's mind the passage in Pringle, read in 1837, which he said[62] he used as the basis for the "hungry lion" figure in *Locksley Hall*.

The familiar "Better fifty years of Europe than a cycle of Cathay" reminds us of the great emphasis Tennyson in his poem puts upon science, the intellect, and the "march of mind" (see the long passage quoted above from *Locksley Hall*). Carlyle, though to a less degree, emphasizes them also (*e.g.*, pp. 1, 60, 102-04), and has Teufelsdröckh declare (p. 143): "In our busy Europe, is there not an everlasting demand for Intellect, in the chemical, mechanical, political, religious, educational, commercial departments?"

Tennyson has his young speaker (ll. 69-75) strive for a moment to be happy—to have "comfort"—but then has him brush aside the desire for comfort. So Teufelsdröckh had discovered (pp. 146-47) that Soul is not Stomach, that physical and mental happiness, *i. e.*, selfish comfort, is not a worthy goal: "This I know, If what thou namest Happiness be our true aim, then we are all astray."

Although not all possible parallels have been pointed out, a sufficient number, I believe, have been indicated, and the case may rest.

We know that before 1842 Tennyson had been greatly interested in German language and literature.[63] Such an interest may have been in part aroused by Carlyle. At any rate, Tennyson's interest in German would not turn him *away* from the story of Teufelsdröckh. Once reading it, he would meet the challenging and yearning statement, at the end of the first chapter: "*Möchte es* (this remarkable Treatise) *auch im Brittischen Boden gedeihen!*" It looks to me as if, a British poet writing for

---

[62] See above, Note 16. Of course a first reading by Tennyson of *Sartor* may have been made before he read Pringle.
[63] See *Memoir*, I, 124; and Teeling, *op. cit.*

the British, he did read the story of the Teufelsdröckh-Blumine affair, accept the challenge quoted above, and rebuild the story into Tennysonian verse of such quality that *Locksley Hall* has indeed thriven in British places.

Writing of Lincolnshire, Walters says that the old hall at North Somercotes appears to have supplied at least one detail for the poet's picture in *Locksley Hall,* the ivied casement; and that "on the authority of the late Rev. Dr. Wood, Tennyson is said to have actually written part of the poem in its ivied casement." He further declares that the poem "was the result of six weeks' continuous labour,"[64] where or when he does not say. Now a letter from Tennyson to Edward FitzGerald indicates that he spent some weeks in 1841 at Mablethorpe on the Lincolnshire coast.[65] It seems to me, putting various details together, that Tennyson wrote *Locksley Hall* after his 1837 reading of Pringle, after his beginning to live near London, dated 1838 in the *Memoir,* and after considerable knowledge of Carlyle, probably personal as well as literary. On the testimony of the Carlyles' correspondence, as well as all the other available evidence, it seems that the poem was completed, very much in its final form, during the spring and summer of 1841. And if it should appear that the poem is indeed the result of six weeks' continuous labor, then it seems probable that Tennyson wrote with *Sartor Resartus* more or less continuously on his desk. Certain it seems, furthermore, that whether or not *Locksley Hall* came from continuous composition Tennyson completed the poem only after he had spent much time in close pondering over the biography of Diogenes Teufelsdröckh.

This study has made clear a broad and deep significance for Tennyson's poem; henceforth a reading of *Locksley Hall* may remind us that its theme is Carlyle's in Book II of *Sartor Resartus,* namely, "Know thy work, in this present age of unrest

[64] Walters, *In Tennyson Land.* . . . , *op. cit.,* pp. 21, 23.
[65] *Memoir,* I, 178.

and injustice and new science and human potentialities, and set about doing that work!" The poem is recognized for a presentation of the social ideal as something that can be moved toward by human energy, the energy of every individual human being. It is clear that Tennyson presents the social and the individual need for every person's becoming a Hero, insofar as that one poor person can—the need of society (as well as each person) for the individual member to act according to the Greatest-Nobleness Principle, not the Greatest-Happiness. Thanks to Tennyson's genius, *Locksley Hall* is a poem that gives an effective illustration of Carlyle's romantic philosophizing in *Sartor*, and gives it in such an enriched way as to defy a charge of plagiarism; it is a vigorous poetical composition bringing local habitation and a familiar terminology to what many readers have found to be relatively "airy nothing" in Carlyle's book. *Locksley Hall* as it may now be understood has brought new life and vigor and applicability to the narrative and to the symbolism of the troubles of Diogenes Teufelsdröckh; the story of the Everlasting Yea has been made Tennysonian English, and the reader who appreciates the transplanting becomes, more than ever before, consciously alive to its intellectual and emotional universality.

Arthur Waugh once declared[66] that it is in the very arguing down of doubt that the power and permanence of Tennyson's poetry lies, such arguing down of doubt as is done, he said, in *Locksley Hall*. For all who agree wholly or in part with Waugh, how great is Tennyson's debt to Carlyle if, as the evidence indicates, he read and absorbed and used the story of Teufelsdröckh's love affair, with its Everlasting No gradually being argued into its Everlasting Yea! The impress of *Sartor* upon one of Tennyson's most long-famous poems makes even stronger the great influence Carlyle wielded over the nineteenth century. Like a Colossus he bestrode the century, someone has said. Now more than before there sounds the ring of solid truth in Matthew

---

[66] Arthur Waugh, *Alfred, Lord Tennyson. A Study of His Life and Work* (New York, 1892), p. 86.

Arnold's tribute[67] to the Sage of Chelsea: "Mr. Carlyle, a man of genius to whom we have all at one time or other been indebted for refreshment and stimulus."

[67] Matthew Arnold, *Culture and Anarchy*, "Doing as One Likes," paragraph 16. Charles Tennyson's *Alfred Tennyson* (New York, 1949) does not disturb the contentions of the present study, written before that book appeared.

WILLIAM DARBY TEMPLEMAN

The University of
Southern California

III

Dickens and the Daily News
The Origin of the Idea

FROM MARCH, 1844, UNTIL JUNE, 1846, inclusive—a period of twenty-eight months—Dickens was concerned with the fortunes of the *Daily News,* as one of its founders, then as its first editor, and finally as a contributor. The origin of the idea of the new daily newspaper has been obscured by the silence of those who knew the facts best. Joseph Hatton, writing in 1881, could say in truth, "Among the stories of the projection and establishment of London papers, that of *The Daily News* has never been completely told."[1] Justin McCarthy and Sir John R. Robinson were able to do no more than to suggest that the general idea of the new liberal paper originated with Dickens and was communicated by him to others. They said:

> Whether the idea was his own to begin with is not easy to find out; but the probability would seem to be that the project came up in his mind, and that he then took other men into his confidence. Some other men having first started the idea would hardly have been likely to think of Dickens as one who would care to undertake the editorship of a daily newspaper, with all its incessant work and supervision and watchfulness.[2]

[1] *Journalistic London* (London, 1881), p. 49.
[2] *"The Daily News" Jubilee, a Political and Social Retrospect of Fifty Years of the Queen's Reign* (London, 1896), p. 4.

Typical of the misunderstanding and misstatement of Dickens' relations to the founding of the *Daily News* is the statement of T. H. S. Escott, in his *Masters of English Journalism,* which leaves the impression that the paper was Dickens' idea of revenge against Sir John Easthope, proprietor of *The Morning Chronicle,* for whom Dickens had worked as a Parliamentary reporter. Escott wrote:

> In 1844 Charles Dickens, whose novels now brought him high praise and world wide fame, renewed, as an occasional writer, his connection with the *Morning Chronicle,*[3] in which, ten years before, he had begun as a reporter[4]. He wanted comparative rest and foreign change. Would the paper commission him to send sketches of European travel from such particular places and at such particular times as he should find convenient? Editor Black[5] had now been succeeded by Andrew Doyle[6]; he, after consultation with his proprietors, found himself compelled to decline the offer on the ground of expenses. Dickens went off in a huff, and never entered the *Chronicle* offices again.[7] The wound inflicted on his self-love refused healing, and would, indeed, give him no rest till he should have started an opposition to his old paper. His special counsellor, John Forster, was called in, arranged a meeting with his publishers, Bradbury and Evans; these at once entered into the proposal.
>
> The capital found for the paper by the printers, Bradbury and Evans, was largely increased by contributions from the novelist's personal friends. . . . All of these now mentioned were influenced personally by Dickens to support the paper. Without his name the

---

[3] Dickens joined the staff of *The Morning Chronicle* at the beginning of the Parliamentary session of 1834, and left it in November, 1836, to become the first editor of *Bentley's Miscellany.*

[4] Escott is in error here. Formerly, it was thought that Dickens began his reportorial career on *The True Sun,* August 7, 1832, but I have shown that in all probability he began, as he himself says, when he was about eighteen, which would have been in 1830, on the staff of his uncle's *Mirror of Parliament.* See Gerald Giles Grubb, "Dickens' First Experience as a Parliamentary Reporter," *The Dickensian,* XXXVI (1940), 211-218.

[5] John Black (1783-1855), editor of *The Morning Chronicle* from 1812-1843.

[6] Doyle was Easthope's son-in-law for whom, without cause, the latter forced Black to resign his editorship in his sixtieth year. This injustice was long remembered among London newspaper men.

[7] These events, of which we here have a garbled account, occurred about March 10, 1844; nevertheless, Sir John Easthope, his wife, and his sister dined at Charles Dickens' table in June just prior to the latter's departure for Italy, in July, 1844.

necessary funds would not have been forthcoming. *The Daily News,* therefore, seemed to him a thing of his own creation, to be dealt with exactly as suited his convenience and whim. He had done his part when he gave the start and drew up the programme, pledging its support to the principles of progress, improvement, of civil and religious liberty, and of equal legislation. That done, in the exercise of his paternal right, he put it out to edit just as, in his novel, Oliver Twist had been put out for an apprentice. Genius resented the drugery of editorship. . . . After four months Forster became in title as well as in reality, the editor of the *Daily News*.[8]

I wish to call special attention to the statements contained in this excerpt from Escott. First, he says or suggests that Dickens was rejected as a leader-writer by the editor of *The Morning Chronicle;* second, that he went away revolving in his mind schemes of vengeance against that newspaper; third, that the whole idea behind the *Daily News* was Dickens'; fourth, that he was acting in a spirit of revenge when he supposedly launched the new paper; fifth, that much of the capital for the enterprise was raised among Dickens' personal friends in response to his personal influence; and sixth, that John Forster was the real editor through the trying days of the new paper's beginning.

Now, if Escott's statement represented the isolated opinion of one man, it would not be worth our time to refute it; but it happens to be in accord, in the main, with the expressed opinions of many of Dickens' biographers.[9]

Dr. Charles Mackay, an interested observer and friend of both Dickens and Sir John Easthope, and at one time a sub-editor of *The Morning Chronicle,* made a statement which shows clearly that Easthope himself was responsible for some of the gossip which Escott and others have printed as facts. Mackay said:

[8] (London, 1911), pp. 211-213.
[9] See A. W. Ward, *Dickens* (New York, 1882), pp. 73-74; Ralph Straus, *Charles Dickens: A Biography from New Sources* (New York, 1928), pp. 215-219; E. E. Kellett, "The Press," in *Early Victorian Period,* edited by G. M. Young (London, 1934), I, 27-28; Thomas Wright, *The Life of Charles Dickens* (New York, 1936), p. 178; and, in some particulars, Una Pope-Hennessy, *Charles Dickens, 1812-1870* (New York, 1946), pp. 230-238.

Sir John Easthope, the chief proprietor of the *Chronicle,* affected not to fear the opposition, declaring that Dickens, anxious above all things to write political leaders for the *Chronicle,* had been found so woefully wanting in political knowledge and tact, as to have rendered it necessary to decline his further services in that capacity. Sir John affirmed to the end of his life that the brilliant author was so greatly offended with the *Morning Chronicle* for its want of judgment, that he set up the *Daily News* as a rival, and that if the conductors of the old journal had had greater appreciation of the genius of the rising novelist the new journal would never have come into existence. Sir John, however, stood alone in his opinion.[10]

People who were undoubtedly friendly toward Dickens have been at a loss to explain his relations with the *Daily News*. In almost every instance his friendly critics and biographers have written of the affair in distinctly apologetic language. It will be sufficient to introduce the statements of two writers who may be taken as typical of many others. Dr. Charles Mackay said:

> Charles Dickens had had more than enough of night-work when engaged in the parliamentary corps of the *Morning Chronicle,* and found the partial renewal of late hours of work in the editorial room of the *Daily News* a little too much for his health and a great deal too much for his comfort. Accordingly, after but short trial of its inconveniences, he transferred his burden to the competent shoulders of his friends, John Forster of the *Examiner* and William Henry Wills, who graduated in the office of *Chamber's Edinburgh Journal.*[11]

Richard Henry Stoddard's statement is popular in style and represents the current opinion that has existed in America even to the present day. Stoddard says:

> Dickens' friends very soon saw that he had taken a false step. The duties of a daily political paper were not suitable to him, and before

[10] Charles Mackay, *Through the Long Day, or, Memories of a Literary Life During Half A Century,* (London, 1887), I, 344.

[11] Mackay, *Through The Long Day,* I, 348. Also see Justin McCarthy and John R. Robinson, *"The Daily News" Jubilee* (London, 1896), pp. 7-8; R. Shelton Mackenzie, *The Life of Charles Dickens* (Philadelphia, 1870), pp. 176-178; Frank T. Marzials, *Life of Dickens* (London, 1887), pp. 99-100; George Saintsbury, "Dickens," *CHEL*, XIII, 359; G. K. Chesterton, "Charles Dickens," *Ency. Brit.*, 14th ed., VII, 334; and Frederic G. Kitton, *Charles Dickens. His Life, Writings, and Personality* (Edinburgh, n.d.), pp. 142-149.

many months he relinquished the editorship, and retired from participation in the "Daily News"—but not, it is understood, without a considerable loss of money.[12]

A careful reading of Forster's *Life of Charles Dickens*,[13] which was published within a few months after the death of Dickens, shows that enough of the truth has been attainable ever since 1871 to refute the most extravagant statements quoted above. To Forster's account of the *Daily News* affair there has been added much new evidence during the last decade. It is now my purpose to analyse Forster's statements and the new documents that have been recently published.

Forster briefly outlines the series of events that led up to Dickens' participation in the establishment of the *Daily News*. In the early months of 1844, certain articles contributed by Dickens to *The Morning Chronicle* on the general subject of slavery and polite society expressed his views in what was then thought to be radical language. The articles aroused a great deal of popular comment, and in reference to them Forster says:

Some articles thus contributed by him having set people talking, the proprietors of the paper rather eagerly mooted the question what payment he would ask for contributing regularly; and ten guineas an article was named. Very sensibly, however, the editor [Andrew Doyle] who had succeeded his old friend Black pointed out to him, that though that sum would not be refused in the heat of the successful articles just contributed, yet (I quote his own account in a letter of the 7th of March, 1844) so much would hardly be paid continuously; and thereupon an understanding was come to, that he would write as a volunteer and leave his payment to be adjusted to the results.[14]

---

[12] Richard Henry Stoddard, *Anecdote Biographies of Thackeray and Dickens*, Bric-a-Brac Series (New York, 1874), p. 221.

[13] Originally published in London by Chapman and Hall, 1871-1872. Numerous editions and reprints have since been issued by various publishers. Best edition: J. W. T. Ley (ed.), *The Life of Charles Dickens by John Forster* (London, 1928).

[14] Ley, *The Life of Charles Dickens by John Forster*, p. 325; Vide, Walter Dexter (ed.), *The Letters of Charles Dickens, The Nonesuch Dickens* (London, 1938), I, 577.

There are two reasons why this letter of March 7, 1844, from Dickens to Forster is of importance. First, it refutes Easthope's charge that Dickens' services as a leader writer were declined by *The Morning Chronicle*, and that as a matter of wounded pride and desire for revenge Dickens founded a paper of his own to compete with Easthope's. Second, mention was made in this letter of a council between Dickens and Bradbury and Evans, the publishers. This council momentously affected the editorial career of Dickens. His letter, quoted by Forster, follows:

Then said the editor—and this I particularly want you to turn over in your mind, at leisure—supposing me to go abroad, could I contemplate such a thing as the writing of a letter a week under any signature I chose, with such scraps of descriptions and impressions as suggested themselves to my mind? If so, would I do it for the *Chronicle?* And if so again, what would I do it for? He thought for such contributions Easthope would pay anything. I told him that the idea had never occurred to me; but that I was afraid he did not know what the value of such contributions would be. He repeated what he had said before; and I promised to consider whether I could reconcile it to myself to write such letters at all. The pros and cons need to be very carefully weighed. I will not tell you to which side I incline, but if we should disagree, or waver on the same points, we will call Bradbury and Evans to the council. I think it more than probable that we shall be exactly of the same mind, but I want you to be in possession of the facts and therefore send you this rigmarole.[15]

---

[15] Forster, *op. cit.*, p. 325. Confirming the truth of the statements made in this March 7th letter, stands the letter Dickens wrote to his solicitor, Thomas Mitton, on March 10, 1844, in which he set forth both the question of the leaders and that of the travel letters. He said: "Easthope is such a damn screw, and it is so impossible to fix him to anything, that I thought it best not to dally, but to do something. . . So I said to Doyle, 'I won't make any bargain with him at all, or haggle like a peddler, but I'll write a leader now and then, and leave him in June to send me a cheque for the whole. He shall set his own value on them; and if he sets too little, the shame is his, and not mine.' He would pay ANY THING, he says, for letters from Italy, but that wouldn't do. I have no doubt he would pay 20 guineas a week. But it wouldn't do." Frederick G. Kitton, *The Minor Writings of Charles Dickens, A Bibliography and a Sketch* (London, 1900), pp. 96-97.

Before examining Forster's reaction to the letter quoted above, I would call attention to the interesting fact that it was the editor of *The Morning Chronicle* who made the original suggestion that Dickens contribute travel letters to his newspaper. This idea lived on in the mind of Dickens and bore fruits almost two years later in the *Pictures from Italy,* originally contributed to the *Daily News.*

Forster, in stating his objection to Editor Doyle's suggestion, said that the "germ" from which the *Daily News* grew was planted in the council suggested in Dickens' letter. It is just here that Forster's comment is of supreme interest. He said:

> The rigmarole is not unimportant; because, though we did not differ on the wisdom of saying No to the *Chronicle,* the 'council' spoken of was nevertheless held, and in it lay the germ of another newspaper enterprise he permitted himself to engage in twelve months later, to which he would have done more wisely to have also answered No.[16]

This statement makes it evident that in all probability Bradbury and Evans, the publishers, had a larger part in the origination of the idea of a daily paper than has heretofore been admitted. Furthermore, Forster spoke of Dickens' saying "No" to the proposal made by the *Chronicle,* and leaves the impression that Bradbury and Evans thereupon made him a proposal of their own to join them in the publication of a newspaper, to which proposition he regretted that Dickens did not also answer No.

The next passage in which Forster mentioned the newspaper project furnishes further evidence that he became aware during the mid-summer months of 1845 that Dickens was considering the possibility of taking a hand in the new venture. Forster said that just as Dickens was wrestling with "The Cricket,"

> ... everything was swept away by a larger scheme, in its extent and its danger more suitable to the wild and hazardous enterprises of that prodigious year (1845) of excitement and disaster. In this more tremendous adventure, already hinted at on a previous page,

---

[16] Forster, *op. cit.,* p. 325.

we all became involved. . . . The change he thus announced to me about half way through the summer, in the same letter which told me the success of d'Orsay's kind exertion to procure a fresh engagement for his courier Roche.¹⁷

This letter of Count d'Orsay's, written, according to Forster's footnote, from "Gore House, 6 July, 1845," fixes the approximate date on which Forster learned that Dickens was definitely turning toward the newspaper project. It is not likely that more than a few days elapsed between this date and that on which Dickens informed Forster of both his inclinations toward the newspaper and his letter from d'Orsay. Walter Dexter, who bases his inference on the Dickens-Beard correspondence,¹⁸ thinks that Dickens confided his ideas about the establishment of a newspaper first to Thomas Beard. However, Dickens' first letter to Beard on the subject—filled with blind questions which did not make his purpose plain at all—was written exactly one month after d'Orsay wrote his note to Dickens, and if Forster was informed about the impending change "about half way through the summer" he must have learned of it in July before the Beard letter was written, which was on August 6th.

At least five considerations must be placed against the suggestion of Escott and others that Dickens originated the idea of the *Daily News*.

Our first consideration is the revelation made by Miss Violet Rose Markham that in the "council" mentioned by Forster in

---

¹⁷ *Ibid.*, p. 379.
¹⁸ Walter Dexter (ed.), *Dickens to His Oldest Friend: The Letters of A Lifetime from Charles Dickens to Thomas Beard* (London and New York, 1933), p. 96. The August 6th letter follows:
"Will you tell me (in the strictest confidence of course) what is the gross expense of the Foreign Department of the Herald: expenses, correspondents' salaries, and everything included, for any given period that may be fairly taken as representing a portion of the round year. And will you tell me, over and above, how much more you may suppose it to be in amount than the similar expenses of our friend the great Baronet [Sir John Easthope, principal owner of *The Morning Chronicle*].
"It seems an odd question, but I will tell you bye and bye how it came about." *Vide*, the Nonesuch Dickens, Letters, I, 691.

the passage quoted above from his *Life*, Bradbury and Evans were not acting for themselves alone. Miss Markham's study of the life and correspondence of Sir Joseph Paxton makes it apparent that Sir Joseph was, if not actually the chief motive force, certainly one of the main personalities behind the whole idea of a new daily paper. In her research for her book entitled *Paxton and the Bachelor Duke*,[19] Miss Markham had access to the private correspondence of Paxton and his wife Sarah. The correspondence covers the whole period of his connection with the *Daily News*. He is portrayed as a man of inordinate ambition who would bear no interference with his cherished plans. One of his fondest ambitions, according to Miss Markham, was to become a successful journalist. In 1831, he became the proprietor and editor of a gardening paper called the *Horticultural Register*, and in the conducting of this journal, he made the acquaintance of William Bradbury of the Bradbury and Evans publishing firm.[20] In 1834, he undertook the conduct of the more ambitious journal entitled the *Magazine of Botany*. Again, in 1841, with his friend Dr. Lindley, Paxton established *The Gardner's Chronicle*, a weekly paper that was still being published when Miss Markham wrote in 1935.[21] About this time Bradbury was printing Paxton's *Magazine of Botany*, and Paxton was advising Bradbury how to invest wisely in railway stocks.

Referring to Paxton's part in the establishment of the *Daily News*, Miss Markham said, "Paxton, like many successful men of business, itched to run a daily paper."[22] She gave him full credit for launching the *Daily News* and for being the pioneer spirit in the enterprise. "He launched," she said, "a powerful journal on its course; hoisted a flag around which great causes gathered."[23] There is no suggestion in Miss Markham's entire

[19] (London, 1935).
[20] Markham, *Paxton*, p. 36.
[21] *Ibid.*, p. 165.
[22] *Ibid.*, p. 168.
[23] *Ibid.*, p. 168.

account of the launching of the *Daily News* that the idea originated with Dickens. In fact, as she proceeded, she made it plain that the idea had its origin in the relations of Paxton with Bradbury.

On October 28, 1845, Dickens wrote a letter to Bradbury and Evans which confirms beyond doubt the truth of Miss Markham's contention that Paxton was the leading figure in the establishment of the *Daily News*. This letter gives a picture of Paxton in action before there had been any announcement of the forthcoming newspaper, and before Dickens became committed to the fortunes of the same. Also, the picture is in thorough accord with the impulsive character Miss Markham portrays in her biography. To Bradbury and Evans, Dickens wrote in a manner that leaves no doubt that it was Paxton and they who were seeking to advance the project, and that Dickens wished them to restrain Paxton's hand. He said:

I really think it very necessary (let me say so while I think of it) that you should privately represent to Mr. Paxton the serious consequences that may come from such loose, flurried way of proceeding as in the case of that Sir George Sargent the other day. To whom the whole thing has been prematurely broached, at a disadvantage, without a point the size of a pin's head being gained. It would be injurious to anything, but to a newspaper it is death.[24]

Our second consideration may well be the evidence of Dickens' reluctance to take part in the founding of a new daily paper. Although he had been giving the newspaper project a great deal of thought,[25] it was not until October 31, 1845, that he wrote to Forster saying that his Christmas story "was at a dead lock"

[24] *The Nonesuch Dickens, Letters*, I, 711-712.
[25] As evidence of Dickens' growing interest in the paper, we have his letter of October 26th, in which he said to Beard:
"Resolve me this question.—Those small correspondents at Madras, Ceylon, and Aden—do they make separate parcels of their newspapers, addressed to the agent at Malta: or do they open the parcel on its way from Calcutta and put them in it? If so, how is the parcel addressed when it leaves Calcutta?—To the agent at the next place? This seems to me to be a query essential to the right working of things." *The Nonesuch Dickens, Letters*, I, 710.

and that he ". . . never was in such bad writing cue." Then Forster made one of his significant but guarded statements about the progress of the newspaper project: "The reason was not far to seek. In the preparation for the proposed new Daily Paper to which reference has been made, he was actively assisting, and had all but consented to the publication of his name." [26]

In this guarded statement two points stand out. (1) "In the preparation for the new Daily Paper . . . he was actively assisting." These words suggest that there were others who were at that time taking the lead in the project—we now know that Forster referred to Paxton and Bradbury and Evans—and that up until October 31, Dickens was only "assisting" them. It is also natural to suppose that he was assisting those who made the original proposal in the council some months earlier. (2) On October 31, he "had all but consented to the publication of his name." It is further evident that pressure from without was being brought to bear upon him to use his name, the name that had proved popular when associated with the editorship of *Bentley's Miscellany* and *Master Humphrey's Clock*. Dickens' reluctance to have the projected newspaper go forward under his name is charged with significance when one remembers that he was willing and anxious to take advantage of his popular name in the case of *Bentley's* and *Master Humphrey*, and that when he was considering the founding of a periodical to be called "The Cricket" he said that it was a title "which people would readily and pleasantly connect with *me*."[27] When he drew his plans for the projected periodical to be called "The Shadow" he again depended upon the popularity of his name to carry his project through. When in 1849, Dickens was considering the establishment of the journal which he owned in the major part and edited from 1850 to 1859, he did not hesitate to associate his name with it, but actually at one time proposed to call it "CHARLES DICKENS. A weekly journal designed for the in-

[26] Forster, *op. cit.*, p. 385.
[27] *Ibid.*, p. 379.

struction and entertainment of all classes of readers. CONDUCTED BY HIMSELF."[28] Finally, it is well known to what immediate purpose he used his name in the titles *Household Words, A Weekly Journal . . . Conducted by Charles Dickens,* and *All the Year Round, A Weekly Journal . . . Conducted by Charles Dickens.* Furthermore, he allowed his name to be thus associated with these journals in advertisements while they were still in the formative stages, months before the publication of their first numbers.[29] Therefore, the most plausible answer to the question of why Dickens was slow in granting the influence of his name to the proposed new paper is that as late as October 31, he was not fully committed to the establishment of the *Daily News.*

On November 1, 1845, Dickens wrote Forster and asked him for a conference. This date may be fixed definitely by Forster's reference to the letter of October 31st. He said, "The morning after his last note I heard again."[30] Now, this "morning after" letter of November 1st, is of interest, for it furnishes strong evidence that neither the conception nor the initiative in the founding of the *Daily News* can be attributed to Dickens. The pertinent part of the letter follows:

I have been so very unwell this morning . . . that I didn't get up until noon: and, shunning Fleet Street (the office of the proposed new paper) [The words in parenthesis are Forster's.] am now going for a country walk, in the course of which you will find me, if you feel disposed to come away in the carriage that goes to you with this . . . There is much I should like to discuss, if you can manage it.[31]

The most significant thing in this letter is Dickens' avoidance of Fleet Street, and Forster's interpolated explanation that "Fleet Street" was "(the office of the proposed new paper)." It shows

[28] *Ibid.,* p. 513.
[29] *Vide, The Athenaeum,* 1157 (December 29, 1849), 1323; *Ibid.,* 1165 (February 23, 1850), 195; *The Illustrated London News,* XVI (March 2, 1850), 151; and *The Saturday Review,* VII (March 26, 1859), 384.
[30] Forster, *op. cit.,* p. 385.
[31] *Ibid.,* p. 385.

that before Dickens had decided to undertake the editorship of the *Daily News,* before he had given the project the use of his name, and before he had postponed the appearance of his Christmas story *The Cricket,* some person or group of persons was forging ahead with plans for a new daily paper. Since "It was at 'No 90,' [Fleet Street] ... in a back room on the second floor ... that most of the preliminaries of the production of *The Daily News* took place ... ,"[32] and since this was the location of the printing establishment of Bradbury and Evans, it is only reasonable to suppose that it was Bradbury and Evans, backed by Paxton and perhaps others, who were the moving spirits in the enterprise. This statement also shows that the originators of the idea had already fitted up a temporary "office of the proposed paper" before Dickens became definitely committed to the project. It suggests, further, that Dickens wished to avoid contact with those who were urging him to undertake the editorship of "the proposed new paper."

After a comment on Dickens' health, Forster mentions the fact that he wrote Dickens a letter in reply to that quoted above.

> His health, however, had no real prominence in my letter; and it is strange now to observe that it appears as an argument in his reply. I had simply put before him, in the strongest form, all the considerations drawn from his genius and fame that should deter him from the labour and responsibility of a daily paper, not less than from the party and political involvements incident to it; and here was the material part of the answer made.[33]

To this letter filled with sound advice, Dickens replied, setting forth some of the considerations that led him to undertake the editorship of the *Daily News.* He wrote:

> Many thanks for your affectionate letter, which is full of generous truth. These considerations weigh with me, *heavily*: But I think I descry in these times, greater stimulants to such an effort; greater chance of some fair recognition of it; greater means of preserving

---

[32] McCarthy and Robinson, *"The Daily News" Jubilee,* p. 6.
[33] Forster, *op. cit.,* p. 386.

in it, or retiring from it unscratched by any weapon one would care for; than at any other period. And most of all I have, sometimes, that possibility of failing health or fading popularity before me, which beckons me to such a venture when it comes within my reach. At the worst, I have written to little purpose, if I cannot *write myself right* in peoples' minds, in such a case as this.[34]

It is hardly to be supposed that Dickens, with his strong belief in his own plans, entering upon the consummation of his own idea, would have from the very beginning considered the possibility of "retiring from it unscratched by any weapon one would care for," if his hopes in it failed to materialize.

Our third consideration will be a refutation of the suggestion of McCarthy and Robinson that "Some other men having first started the idea would hardly have been likely to think of Dickens as one who would care to undertake the editorship of a daily newspaper . . ."[35] This suggestion will not hold up when closely examined in the light of the popularity of Dickens in 1845 and 1846. Theirs is a judgment passed in retrospect and based upon a superficial knowledge of Dickens' methods and policies as an editor. To a firm of publishers and a group of business men looking forward to the establishment of a liberal daily newspaper, Dickens had more to recommend him than almost any other mid-Victorian who was not already attached to some leading sheet. (1) He was recognized by competent judges as the best newspaper reporter of his generation.[36] (2) He had been trained under the great editor, John Black of *The*

[34] *Ibid.*, p. 386.
[35] McCarthy and Robinson, *op. cit.*, p. 4.
[36] James Grant, one of Dickens' contemporaries in the gallery, said of him, ". . . he occupied the very highest rank of the eighty or ninety reporters for the press then in Parliament." *The Newspaper Press* (London, 1871), I, 296. Charles Mackay, one time sub-editor of *The Morning Chronicle*, referred to Dickens and Beard as "the two best reporters of their day." Dexter, *Dickens-Beard Letters*, p. xvii. Again Mackay said "Among the parliamentary reporters was Mr. Thomas Beard, who always ran in harness with Mr. Dickens whenever there was special or extraordinary work to be done. . ." *Fifty Years Recollection of Life, Literature, and Public Affairs, From 1830-1870* (London, 1877), I, 82. *Vide*, Gerald Giles Grubb, "Charles Dickens: Journalist," Typewritten Dissertation, The University of North Carolina, 1940, pp. 11-92.

Morning Chronicle, sometimes called, as Frederic G. Kitton remarked, "the 'Father' of the London Press."[37] (3) His journalistic enterprises—*Sketches by Boz* and *Pickwick Papers*—had already made him the most popular writer of his time. (4) He had successfully inaugurated *Bentley's Miscellany* and edited it for two years. (5) He had written and edited *Master Humphrey's Clock,* a weekly periodical, doubtless equal to the editing of a daily newspaper. (6) It was known that he possessed a large circle of friends engaged in journalism of all descriptions; and his experience as editor of *Bentley's* had shown that he could surround himself with an efficient, even distinguished, staff. (7) His associations had been exclusively with liberal periodicals, newspapers, and editors;[38] and it was known that he was actively interested in reform. (8) Bradbury and Evans as his publishers, through the council mentioned by Forster, knew that Dickens was at least attracted by the idea of becoming editor of a newspaper. (9) His name alone—even if he were editor in name only—was of no small value in the successful floating of a new daily newspaper. These qualifications should have made Dickens in 1845 a promising candidate for the editorship of a daily newspaper.

For our fourth consideration, arises the question: If Dickens was the originator and original moving spirit in the founding of the *Daily News,* why was his attitude toward the ownership of the property unparalleled in any other enterprise of like nature in which he was ever interested? He is supposed, by some, to have originated the *Daily News,* but he did not own it, or any share in it. On the other hand, he retained what amounted to practical control of the property of those publications which were of his own origination. *Pickwick* grew from the ideas of

---

[37] *Charles Dickens, His Life, Writings, and Personality* (New York, 1908) p. 31.

[38] Dickens' connections—sometimes very brief—with publications prior to 1845 had been as follows: *The Mirror of Parliament, The True Sun, The Morning Chronicle, The Evening Chronicle, The Monthly Magazine, Bell's Life in London, The Library of Fiction, Carlton Chronicle, Bentley's Miscellany,* and his own one-man periodical, *Master Humphrey's Clock.*

Chapman and Hall; likewise, *Bentley's Miscellany* was a product of the ideas of the Bentleys; and neither belongs in the category of his originations. But he retained control of *Master Humphrey's Clock*, and in his abortive plans for "The Cricket"[39] and "The Shadow"[40] he expected to retain practical control. He was careful to retain control of *Household Words*;[41] and in the case of *All the Year Round*, he retained control not only of the tangible property, but of the title also.[42] Why should he have departed so sharply from his general policy, in the case of the proprietorship of the *Daily News*, if the idea had originated with him? The obvious answer is that the *Daily News* was not his idea originally, and that he was paid a salary to perfect the ideas of other men.

Fifth, we must consider the fact that we have no evidence that Dickens was acquainted with any of the proprietors before the establishment of the *Daily News* with the exception of the firm of Bradbury and Evans. It is hardly reasonable to suppose that such men as Sir Joseph Paxton, Sir Joshua Walmesley, and Sir William Jackson, whose names appear in all the extant lists of the proprietors,[43] would have responded to Dickens' invitation to form a new paper and turn it over to him without his assumption of a very substantial share of the financial responsibility as

---

[39] Forster, *op. cit.*, pp. 378-379.
[40] *Ibid.*, pp. 511-512.
[41] R. C. Lehmann, *Charles Dickens as Editor, Being Letters Written By Him to William Henry Wills His Sub-Editor* (New York, 1912), p. 19.
[42] Lehmann, *Charles Dickens as Editor*, pp. 261 and 271.
[43] Grant, *The Newspaper Press*, II, 77-78. Thanks to Miss Violet Rose Markham, who had the original partnership agreement that controlled the *Daily News* before her when she wrote, we now know just how that newspaper was financed. The amount of capital subscribed by each of the four original partners was Sir Joseph Paxton, £25,000, William Bradbury and Frederick M. Evans, jointly, £22,500, and Joseph Wright, £2,500. Bradbury and Evans were named managers with the authority to bring in as much extra capital as they thought necessary. Sir Joshua Walmesley and Sir William Jackson were brought in under this elastic clause of the agreement. (*Paxton*, p. 168.) In a prepared statement written on November 7th or 8th, 1845, Dickens referred to "the subscribing parties" and then added "of whom I was never one to the value of a farthing." (*The Nonesuch Dickens, Letters*, I, 718-719.)

a pledge of good faith and continued interest. On the other hand, since Bradbury and Evans and Sir Joseph Paxton were the originators of the idea and the moving spirits in the enterprise, and were at the same time offering to share a large portion of the financial responsibility, it was not hard for them to attract generous supporters.

Finally, the tone and the contents of the letter in which Dickens accepted the editorship of the *Daily News* throw their weight decisively against the notion that Dickens originated the idea of the new paper. It shows, in spite of McCarthy and Robinson's statments, that some other men did originate the idea, did seek Dickens, and did accept hard terms in order to secure his services as editor. It is evident now that it was a case of the job seeking the man, rather than the man seeking the job. Dickens wrote Bradbury and Evans, from Forster's house, on Monday, November 3, 1845, as follows:

> I have given my best consideration to the subject we discussed yesterday; and in this letter you have my conclusions in reference to the newspaper.
> I will take that post of Editor which is marked in the little statement as having a salary of a Thousand Pounds attached to it—for double that salary. In which I include the Publication of the series of Italian letters, with my name—my frequently writing for the paper from day to day—my constantly exercising an active and vigilant superintendence over the whole machine. When I am there, or after I have left the office, I shall, (as the custom is) have a Sub-Editor to whom I can, with perfect confidence, hand over the practical management for the time being. The head and leading principle of the thing I am willing to become on these terms.
> I will not disguise from you—for I am pretty sure you will feel—that I think they are far from high for one in my position. And therefore I make my share in the paper an object of importance. But it is quite impossible that I can say what, in my opinion, that share should be, without your first showing me out of what proportion of the whole it is to come.
> If you feel disposed to do so, on this short statement of the compensation I aim at, you can give this information to Mr. Forster, and

arrange that point, as well as any other, with him. I am fully prepared to abide by any arrangement you agree upon.[44]

To sum up the evidence concerning the origin of the idea of the *Daily News*, the conception and order of events seem to have been as follows: (1) Shortly after March 7, 1844, in a council composed of Bradbury and Evans, Forster, and Dickens, called for the purpose of considering the advisability of Dickens' accepting the invitation of the editor of *The Morning Chronicle* to write travel letters for that sheet, Bradbury and Evans, acting for themselves and Sir Joseph Paxton, advanced the idea of a new daily newspaper with Dickens as its editor. (2) Dickens went away from this council in a state of indecision. (3) Forster protested against the whole scheme; and Dickens, before reaching a decision, began an investigation, in the course of which he wrote to Thomas Beard for certain information. (4) In the meantime, Bradbury and Evans and Paxton had opened an office in Fleet Street and were forming a corporation for the support of the new publication; so far as evidence is now available, the corporation seems to have included persons previously unacquainted with Dickens. (5) Dickens began by "assisting" those who were forming the firm, lost the inspiration for his Christmas story, and on November 3, 1845, gave himself up wholly to the enterprise. (6) He then became a paid employee of the firm, and turned his hand to the task of building a great newspaper.

[44] *The Nonesuch Dickens, Letters*, I, 713-714.

GERALD GILES GRUBB

Wake Forest College

IV
Arnold's Marguerite

THE "PROBLEM" OF Matthew Arnold's Marguerite is by way of becoming as much of a critical nuisance as that of Chaucer's Criseyde. In both there is no final judgment to be had, and it requires therefore a certain boldness to renew the quest (as in the present instance) without fresh and positive evidence. Something may be gained however from reviewing the "case," attempting to distinguish the known facts and the plausible deductions, and thus possibly clarifying the issue.[1]

Marguerite is a problem, first, because so many rash and conflicting statements have been made about her, with a resultant confusion for anyone who might care to ascertain the truth. Yet it would be intolerably tedious, perhaps also presumptuous, to collect these statements and attempt controversially to confute or correct them, and I shall touch as lightly as possible on this part of the subject. But Marguerite is a really important prob-

[1] Since the publication of *Twelve Victorian Authors* in 1936, of Lowry's edition of the letters to Clough in 1932, and of Tinker and Lowry's *The Poetry of Matthew Arnold, A Commentary* in 1940, most of the bibliographical details and important facts for a study of Arnold's poetry have been readily accessible; and therefore the usual references are omitted in the present article. It is perhaps worth adding, however, that the quotation from Mr. T. S. Eliot on p. 81 is from *The Use of Poetry and the Use of Criticism;* that from Stopford Brooke on p. 83 from his *Four Victorian Poets;* that from Professor Garrod on p. 90 from his *Poetry and the Criticism of Life;* and that from Sir E. K. Chambers from his Warton Lecture, 1932. The letter of Mr. Andrew S. Cairncross appeared in *T.L.S.* for 28 March, 1935; the note by Mr. H. M. Walbrook in the London *Bookman* for May, 1930, pp. 109-12. All the other references will be easily identified.

lem in the biography of Arnold—to say nothing of the poetry she inspired, some very good and some less good—because she illuminates that conflict in Arnold's life and character which Professor E. K. Brown has recently studied from quite another point of view in his *Matthew Arnold, A Study in Conflict*. She has a poetical significance and a biographical significance both inescapable and both ramifying in various directions.

I

Readers of Arnold's second volume of verse, *Empedocles on Etna and Other Poems*, 1852 (they were certainly few), when they came to the series of eleven poems beginning on page 73 with "The River" and ending with "To Marguerite" may have noted fragments of a love story: first the distant and hopeless wooing, then the fevered meeting, followed by separation and resignation. And so, it seems reasonable to suppose, Arnold intended the series to be read. The lady's name was Marguerite, and there were sufficient circumstantial details to give the story an air of reality. If there were inconsistencies, they might pass unnoticed: certainly the details were hardly enough to warrant deducing a complete or coherent narrative. And if the incidents were drawn from two separate experiences, *that* would be an irrelevant matter. In point of fact, at least one reader, Mr. Andrew S. Cairncross, more than eighty years later (1935), saw fit to understand these poems as parts of "a single novelette in verse." The two women, he found, were "types, representing passion and ideal love—Marguerite and Urania; ... The leading intention was to contrast the arch mockery and promiscuous passion of Marguerite—*la femme sensuelle moyenne*—with the disillusioned idealism of Urania, and the physical passion of the poet's own nature with his aspiration to spiritual love." And a few years before this, Mr. H. M. Walbrook had suggested that Arnold's Marguerite story was "a *donnée* worth considering" by some properly qualified contemporary in search of material for an idyllic romance. With these speculations I am not concerned, but they would perhaps have gratified Arnold.

When in the next year Arnold published under his full name *Poems. A New Edition* (a selection from his two preceding volumes together with eight new poems), the reader would have missed the first six of the series, the six expressing hopeless love for an inaccessible lady, and would have noted that four of the others, with two new ones, were grouped under the heading "Switzerland." In successive re-editions of his poems Arnold shifted the order and altered the content of this group, until in the *Selected Poems* of 1878 they stood as we now read them. But already in 1853, when the group was set up and the other poems withdrawn, it was clear that Arnold meant to limit the canon of Marguerite poems by the new title and that he did not intend the poems which had formerly preceded them to be read as parts of her "story." He might change the order of the "Switzerland" poems, add to them, or take old ones away, but those which he placed in the "Switzerland" group were manifestly the poems which he wished us to read as Marguerite's poems. (See Note on the Rearrangements of the Poems, page 98, below.)

In 1855, moreover, when he published *Poems. Second Series,* Arnold collected four of the eleven poems which in 1852 looked like a continuous series, and added one new one, under the heading "Faded Leaves": and these were not reprinted until the Collected Edition of 1869, vol. i. Yet in spite of this very marked separation of the two groups by Arnold himself and in spite of the noticeable differences in setting and in descriptive detail, readers and critics have persisted in confusing and even in confounding them; and likewise persisted in adding freely to the Marguerite canon on their own responsibility.

On the other hand, readers and critics of Arnold have been more cautious in assuming the reality of this Marguerite. "It is not easy to decide," said Saintsbury, for example, "and it is perhaps in both senses impertinent to speculate whether the Marguerite of the poems had any live original." Mr. T. S. Eliot has dismissed her as "at best a shadowy figure, neither very passionately desired nor very closely observed, a mere pretext for lamentation." But most of the others have accepted her as real on the evidence of the poems, though usually with some safeguarding phrase. Since the publication of Arnold's letters to Clough (edited by Dr. Lowry in 1932), however, the assumption is strengthened: for on 29 September, 1848 Arnold wrote to Clough, from Leukerbad: "Tomorrow I repass the Gemmi and get to Thun, linger one day at the Hotel Bellevue for the sake of the blue eyes of one of its inmates: and then proceed by slow stages down the Rhine . . . to England." And from Thun, 23 September, 1849 Arnold told Clough: "I wrote to you from this place last year," and in the same letter copied a portion of the Marguerite poem, "A Parting," which he was apparently then composing. In view of this evidence it is difficult to avoid the conclusion that Marguerite was a real person, even in the face of Arnold's reported denial; and such a conclusion, though it is of course based on inference, is further supported by two general considerations. Many of Arnold's poems are occasional in the sense that they took their origin in special circumstances, and the "Switzerland" poems certainly seem to be of this sort: some of them are circumstantial to a degree hardly consistent with fictional invention. Moreover, if the "Switzerland" poems had been intended as fiction Arnold might have been expected to make them less fragmentary and more coherent. One recalls, to be sure, his handling of the Tristram story, which is fragmentary enough, but Arnold was uncomfortable about his "management" of it; and there is no record of his dissatisfaction with the "Switzerland" poems on this ground.

The conclusion then that Marguerite was a real person and that the experience reported in her poems represents a real experience may be regarded as justifiable, but the inferences to be drawn from it are another matter. No one will read the poems as a record which is factually accurate in all details. But one may reconstruct the simple outlines somewhat as follows: Arnold met at Thun in 1848, or a year earlier, a young woman whom in the poems he calls Marguerite and enjoyed a mild flirtation with her—he had not yet settled down, it should be remembered, and begun snuffing after "a moral atmosphere." The next year he returned to Thun, still in love but now disturbed by that anxious choice which agitated his breast so intensely, the choice, phrased variously, between the world and the individual, between the demands of society and the urge to be himself; and this choice now took visible form in Marguerite. Should he give rein to his impulses or obey the God's tremendous voice, with which were perhaps mingled the paternal tones of Dr. Arnold's memory? So he lectures himself and her, finds himself wanting in passion and her in faith, feels exalted and cast down by turns; and then while he is crying Yea and sighing Nay, there appears a stranger with grey eyes which remind him of her blue eyes. This stranger is perhaps the *"unerreichbare schöne"* with whom Arnold fell in love, in the summer of 1850, and whom (after his appointment as inspector of schools had been arranged) he married in June, 1851.

Mr. Walbrook asks a natural question: "Is it credible that if this story of enchantment, jealousy and anguish were one of actual fact, Matthew Arnold of all men would have gone pouring it forth to the public during the early years of his perfectly happy married life? Or that, under any circumstances, he would have committed a Marguerite whom he had not only loved and lost but also, in the bitterness of his disillusionment, harshly analyzed, to the stray speculations of any stranger picking up the book?" To this one can reply that other poets have frequently done much the same thing. There are, for example, Shakespeare in the Sonnets, Byron and Shelley *passim,* and doubtless many another if we possessed all the facts. True, one does not expect this unlocking of his heart by a Victorian poet, but Arnold was never a complete Victorian in the cant sense of that adjective. There is, moreover, an inevitable conflict between the urge to create and the restraints of reticence, and probably each poet has thought of himself as keeping well on the right side of personal revelation. If a case is to be made out against Arnold it would be in connection with the "Faded Leaves" poems, which, however innocuous on moral grounds, are on æsthetic grounds hardly as complimentary as one might wish; and since they add less than a cubit to Arnold's poetic stature one might question the taste of publishing them at all. Or, in other words, if Mrs. Arnold was to be sensitive about Marguerite, what would she think of herself in print, her poems alongside Marguerite's in 1852 and she herself apparently as a grey-eyed "stranger" in one of Marguerite's poems? (It is not impossible that there was even some interchange during the earliest stages of composition between the "Switzerland" and the "Faded Leaves" poems; and in "The Buried Life" there are signs of two different women.) But the fatuity of all such divagations is reached in Stopford Brooke's comment on the "flowery track" stanza of "The Terrace at Berne": "I do not think that the poet could ever have really loved the girl, else the memory of tenderness and of passion would have spared her that conjecture."

II

About the young woman herself we know next to nothing except a few details of her appearance and the fact that she was not the one to determine Arnold's choice. Her pale cheeks "of languid hue," her "soft kerchief'd hair," and particularly "those sweet eyes of blue"; her "clear voice," "buoyant as morning," and her "arch smile"—these are a lover's description and tell us little. It is something perhaps to hear of

> The unconquer'd joy in which her spirit dwells

and to learn that she had embraced other men before Arnold met her and that when he returned to Switzerland she no longer loved him; and also that years afterward he wondered if she had become a Paris prostitute. For the rest, we may take our cue from one who knew her best, and not

> try
> To things by mortal course that live
> A shadowy durability
> For which they are not meant, to give.

The language is crabbed, but it is Arnold's last word about her, his last farewell to her, and the phrase, for the sake of which he gallantly sacrificed both rime and order, is almost a perfect summary. The woman who in 1848 had so moved his "starting, feverish heart," had achieved by 1863, after his marriage and twelve years of school inspecting, after domestic love and the *world* had made their way with him—the young woman whom he called Marguerite had achieved only a *shadowy* durability, a shadowy *durability*.

> Go then!

in one breath; and in the next—

> Stay with me, Marguerite still!

But it is not about Marguerite that we care to know, so much as about her poet. Of the nine poems which can certainly be called hers we cannot establish the dates of composition. We seem to see her first with an Olivia in "A Dream." This is a bit of almost humorously grandiloquent blank verse—

> They saw us, they conferr'd; their bosoms heaved,
> And more than mortal impulse fill'd their eyes.

Then he and his companion Martin are carried past by the "Loud thundering" river of life—which may well be a fanciful extension of the River Aar. The next poem, with its long title, "To My Friends, Who Ridiculed a Tender Leave-Taking," later reduced to "A Memory Picture," is overtly playful and Horatian: they may laugh, but

> I, with little land to stir,
> Am the exacter labourer;

and painting a detailed portrait of her lilac kerchief, soft face, arch chin, pale cheek, and so on, he cherishes the memory of a blithe flirtation. It is a frivolous little poem, what his family expected of him rather than the serious portions of the 1849 volume and was of course properly segregated to the Early Poems (in 1878).

The "Switzerland" group begins with "Meeting," first called rather pointlessly "The Lake" (*i.e.*, Thunersee). He sees Marguerite "again" (and now the printed page refers us by a note to "A Memory Picture" of the preceding year), but as he springs to make his choice he is constrained by "a God's tremendous voice." The significant word is *choice*. Between the tender leave taking and this meeting he has been home and seen the necessity of settling down; now he escapes for a holiday in Switzerland looking for peace, putting ambition behind him, and to the voice and the "Powers who join and part" he answers:

> Ah, warn some more ambitious heart,
> And let the peaceful be.

"Parting" is a companion piece to "Meeting," but it is not so much a parting of lovers as a parting of the ways. He is making his choice between Marguerite and the mountains, between love, all for love, and the romantic solitude which is peace if not comfort. Here we begin to be on firm biographical ground. The letter to Clough of 23 September, 1849 saying, "I wrote to you from this place [Thun] last year" seems to be lost, but that from Leukerbad, 29 September, 1848, helps to fill in certain details. On Wednesday the 27th of September Arnold was at Domodossola immune to the attractions of the *"superbes filles"* seen there by his guide; on Thursday he crossed the Simplon on his way to Leukerbad, where he wrote Friday that he would "repass the Gemmi" the next day. And to *re*pass the Gemmi could only mean return to Thun. Evidently he had been in Thun earlier in the month. In this same letter he speaks disrespectfully of womankind and thus implies that he is already less than completely captivated by Marguerite. "I am glad to be tired of an author [Béranger]: one link in the immense series of cognoscenda and indaganda despatched. More particularly is this my feeling with regard to (I hate the word) women. We know beforehand all they can teach us: yet we are obliged to learn it directly from them."

The next summer he was again on the continent and suggested to Clough a meeting at Geneva early in August. By 23 September he was in Thun once more—how much earlier we do not know—and from the tone of his long letter to Clough then he was evidently far from calm: ". . . these are damned times . . . light profligate friends, moral desperadoes like Carlyle, our own selves. . . ." The particular allusion to Marguerite is as follows: "I am here in a curious and not altogether comfortable state: however tomorrow I carry my aching head to the mountains and to my cousin the Blümlis Alp." And after quoting nine lines from "Parting" he adds: "Yes, I come, but in three or four days I shall be back here, and then I must try how soon I can ferociously turn towards England."

At the same time Arnold was at work also on the first "Obermann" poem, from which he copied out two lines, and he lamented that he had "never yet succeeded in any one great occasion in mastering" himself—"at the critical point I am too apt to hoist up the mainsail to the wind and let her drive"—but he hoped for improvement. Now the "Stanzas in Memory of the Author of 'Obermann'" were "conceived and partly composed," said Arnold in his note to the poem, "in the valley going down from the foot of the Gemmi Pass towards the Rhone"—that is, on the way to Leukerbad. The stanza referring to Wordsworth, he explained in a footnote, was written in November, 1849. (Later he gave the whole poem the subtitle "November 1849.") Our next date is from the letter to Clough written from Rugby in mid-November of this year. The evidence is not altogether satisfactory, but it seems to indicate that he lingered in

Switzerland through October and it might be construed to mean that he fled to the Blümlis Alp more than once while he was making his choice.

In "Parting" the mountains call him, and the voice of Marguerite, real or imagined, detains him. He cries to the mountains "I come"; he takes leave of Marguerite, telling her that their "different past" is a barrier between them and that their "spirits have grown" apart; and he beseeches Nature to calm and restore him. The letter and the poem agree perfectly. Then follows the poem "A Farewell," which does not contain her name and when first published, in 1852, was kept distinct from her other poems, and which, while it fits the chronology, contains some inconsistencies disturbing to the coherence of the story.

It is clear, however, that Arnold was at Thun twice in September, 1848, with an interval in the mountains, and likewise twice in September-October, 1849, with a similar interval in the mountains, at least as far as Leukerbad, escaping from himself and from Marguerite. As "Parting" describes the desire to escape, so "A Farewell" describes his return and final break with Marguerite. They embrace warmly and weep together, "with hearts too full to speak." He had in the preceding poem told himself, but obviously not her, that they were not suited for each other; and he tries again. "Days flew," he reports in the poem, while in terms of the letter he had already written to Clough he was trying ferociously to turn towards England. Days fly and Marguerite becomes cool. But he does not blame her, rather he deplores his own inconstancy and want of "trenchant force"—here one should read the cancelled poem "Destiny"— and he dismisses her, though not without a truculent note, with the prophecy that they will meet in a future life, all passion spent,

> Ennobled by a vast regret,
> And by contrition,

and enjoy the peace which

> a raving world
> Would never let us satiate here.

It is all somewhat Byronic, but it tells us plainly that he has learned not to trust his impulses and not to sacrifice his future for an unstable passion.

These details are, it should go without saying, not to be taken with biographical literalness. But they echo his letters, which in turn add corroborative verisimilitude to his account of Marguerite, and they (letters and poems together) show something of the storm and stress which preceded his surrender to the world only a little more than a year later.

The story ends as Arnold had foreseen. His decision made, he turned towards England, reflecting that

> we forget because we must
> And not because we will;

that he is not exactly calmed and ennobled by his decision, but only chilled by it; and crying—

> Stay with me, Marguerite, still!

But in this very poem, "Absence," he tells of meeting a "fair stranger" with grey eyes who reminds him of Marguerite; and whether by coincidence or by design these may well be the

> Eyes too expressive to be blue,
> Too lovely to be grey,

the grey eyes of the "stranger" of "Faded Leaves," that is to say, of Miss Wightman. If this poem is of the autumn of 1849 and Arnold's courtship of his wife was in the summer of 1850 (which is what the books tell us), the overlapping is a felicitous accident, a poetic rather than a biographic truth. Then ten years pass (a round number) and in 1863 Arnold looks from "The Terrace at Berne" across at his cousin the Blümlis Alp and back to Marguerite. For she is "with him still"—"my Marguerite." He speculates rather harshly on what has become of her; they have met and passed on the sea of life; and this is the end, peace, so far as Marguerite is concerned.

Now we may return and follow the same path through other poems. While Arnold was taking leave of Marguerite and seeking calm in the mountains he found at first only another unrest in the fevered pages of Obermann. In "Parting" he listened for "The mountain bee's hum" and in the Obermann stanzas—

> Yet, through the hum of torrent lone,
> And brooding mountain-bee,
> There sobs I know not what ground-tone
> Of human agony.

And here also he faced his choice:

> Ah! two desires toss about
> The poet's feverish blood.
> One drives him to the world without,
> And one to solitude.

Like the ideal poet in "Resignation" (composed some while before) he believes that

> He who hath watch'd, not shared, the strife,
> Knows how the day hath gone.
> He only lives with the world's life,
> Who hath renounced his own.

So now, in November, 1849, having given up Marguerite he gives up Senancourt (and in the 1852 volume "A Farewell" immediately precedes the "Stanzas")—

> Away the dreams that but deceive,
> And thou, sad guide, adieu!
> I go, fate drives me; but I leave
> Half of my life with you. . . .
>
> I in the world must live

leaving half of his life behind: an unhappy, unwilling choice, also with a poetical sequel. For the *New Poems* (1867) in which he first published "The Terrace at Berne" closes with "Obermann Once More," still with "the wild bee's Alpine hum," though in another part of Switzerland. Here where Arnold for once associates himself with the great Victorian optimism, letting Obermann lament his "frustrate life" and celebrate prophetically the glories of Victorian prosperity, he proclaims himself as

> serene,
> Yet tinged with infinite desire
> For all that *might* have been—
>
> The harmony from which man swerved
> Made his life's rule once more!

The language is perhaps deliberately cryptic and subject to interpretation. It suggests however an imperfect reconciliation, resignation rather than content: the harmony which he had missed long ago and still yearns for. Serene, yes, like the later Matthew Arnold of the essays, and bland and slightly supercilious, but unsatisfied; the "Once-long'd-for storms of love" given over for quiet domestic love and family life, the solitude and contemplation sacrificed for the dusty world and a life of school inspecting, regret and still imperfect harmony for himself.

This conflict, which led to this issue, is bodied forth, moreover, in another poem of the "Empedocles" volume—"Marguerite's book," as Professor Garrod perversely called it; for the inconstant Marguerite is certainly one element of his chaos, but certainly she does not dominate the volume. In "A Summer Night" the moonlight charges him with hesitation between the active life and his own inner desires.

> Hast thou then still the old unquiet breast,
> Which neither deadens into rest,
> Nor ever feels the fiery glow
> That whirls the spirit from itself away,
> But fluctuates to and fro,
> Never by passion quite possess'd
> And never quite benumb'd by the world's sway?

This, it seems to me, sums up perfectly, almost epigrammatically, the mental turmoil of which Marguerite was a part; and at the end of the poem the "silent pain" of those

> Who have long'd deeply once, and long'd in vain

may be an allusion to her share of it—"long'd" notice, not "loved."

The cross-reference in Arnold's notes to "A Southern Night," written in 1859 or 1860, to "A Summer Night" is more puzzling than helpful. The former poem says that the soft moonlight at Cette reminds him of a similar night "of yore" and a trouble now forgotten. The latter poem contains two moonlight pictures, the principal one of moonlight over the housetops of a deserted street, and a subordinate inset picture of a then "past night, and a far different scene," which corresponds fairly closely with the picture in "A Southern Night." Mr. Frederick Page has suggested that the reference is to the Marguerite poem "A Farewell," but this can hardly be so because the details of the inset picture (moonlit deep, spring tide, glistening bay) do not fit the Thunersee background at all; and the principal moonlight picture of "A Summer Night" is so general that it would fit any setting with a street. In any case the figure of Marguerite is dim here.

Nor is she more than a background figure in that rather unexpected outburst in Part III of "Tristram and Iseult"—the "gradual furnace of the world" in which our spirits are withered and our pleasures staled—

> This, or some tyrannous single thought, some fit
> Of passion, which subdues our souls to it, . . .
> Call it ambition, or remorse, or love.

Nor does the intrusive image of Vivian at the end resemble Marguerite save for her blue eyes and what she has in common with the universal *femme fatale*. Vivian's seduction of Merlin and Marguerite's spell over her poet are poles asunder.

Two poems of the "Switzerland" group remain to be considered: they are hardly parts of the story, yet significant elements of the picture. The other poems of the group are but small stars in Arnold's poetic diadem; the "Isolation" poems, in spite of their handicap of shifting and unfortunate titles, are Marguerite's triumph, her immortality, the tokens of her durability. The first, as we now read them, though not published till five years after the other, is perhaps artistically less successful, with its juxtaposition of modern rhetoric—

> The fault was grave! ...
> Thou lov'st no more;—Farewell! Farewell!
>
> Farewell!—and thou, thou lonely heart ...
> Back to thy solitude again!

and the classical picture of Luna and Endymion, and the homiletic note of

> to prove
> This truth—to prove and make thine own;

but the conclusion is near Arnold's lyric best:

> Or, if not quite alone, yet they
> Which touch thee are unmating things—
> Ocean and clouds and night and day;
> Lorn autumns and triumphant springs;
> And life, and others' joy and pain,
> And love, if love, of happier men.
>
> Of happier men—for they, at least,
> Have *dream'd* two human hearts might blend
> In one, and were through faith released
> From isolation without end
> Prolong'd; nor knew, although not less
> Alone than thou, their loneliness.

The other,

> Yes! in the sea of life enisled ...
> The unplumb'd, salt, estranging sea

is Arnold's lyric best, though marred by one or two infelicities.

It is or should be revealing that when the "winds of passionate welcome and farewell" are blown away, the poetic theme of Marguerite's love is isolation—not, as one critic has phrased it, "the spiritual isolation which must ever separate two souls who are respectively involved; the woman in the gay, romantic life of Paris and of Switzerland, the man in the austere service of Faith," but rather the annihilating sense of isolation which overwhelms two lovers (or one of them) at the failure of love, when "their longing's fire" is "as soon as kindled, cool'd" and there is no blending of their hearts or spirits. This is Arnold's secret, if we are to put any trust in his poetic sincerity. In "Destiny" he asked why with

> A heart of ice, a soul of fire

he was always striving

> To love more deeply than he can.

Now he recognizes that Marguerite has not been able to arouse in him such a passion as he would like to feel, that the whole affair is a failure because neither of them was sufficiently moved. In other Marguerite poems he makes his excuses: she was not this, he was not that. But apparently the truth is that he wanted to fall passionately in love, but never quite succeeded because she did not really melt his heart of ice. Afterward, to be sure, as well as during the stress and strain, he cherished the experience since it was the one experience in which he nearly was swept away, as a young man and admirer of Byron would wish to be; which had taught him perhaps that such love was not for him. It was failure on both sides, and its sharpest pressure was that sense of isolation, of the predestined and insuperable barrier between souls which have eagerly desired to unite and could not.

The double irony of the sequel is another matter. For he had no sooner dismissed Marguerite and forsaken Obermann, he had no sooner admitted to himself that love is not enough and that he must accept the world, than he became equally eager to win Miss Wightman, and, that accomplished, he heard the Justice's "tremendous voice" speaking for the world and financial security: a very practical criticism of life. Or in the words of Sir Edmund Chambers:

Certainly the parting with a blue-eyed girl became for Matthew Arnold something more than itself, a parting with the whole world of passionate romance which he put behind him. The Marguerite poems are not merely poems of isolation, but of renunciation, of self-dedication. There had been a κάθαρσις. He turned back to his 'sphered course', to the rigorous teachers who had seized his youth, . . . and incidentally to the routine, which he often found irksome, of the Education Office.

There is some exaggeration in this, and some truth. The Education Office was more than an incident. Marguerite is more than the symbol, less than the whole, of Arnold's conflict when the "worldling" was rapidly maturing into the "prophet." The real note of the Marguerite poems is that of unrealized passion, self-thwarted: a private revelation, a renunciation, and a kind of katharsis. But it was Justice Wightman (so one reads the evidence) who *ab extra* assigned him the lesser rôle of Martha and propelled the poet into a career of self-dedication to culture and, to use the modern word, service.

But after the die was cast it was still difficult to forget. In January, 1851, the year of his marriage, Arnold wrote to his sister K: "The aimless and unsettled, but also open and liberal state of our youth we *must* perhaps all leave and take refuge in our morality and character; but with most of us it is a melancholy passage from which we emerge shorn of so many beams that we are almost tempted to quarrel with the law of nature which imposes it on us." In 1853, already tired of inspecting schools and longing for the restfulness of a diplomatic post, he wrote to his wife: "All this afternoon I have been haunted by a vision of living with you at Berne, on a diplomatic appointment." And the next year: "How I should like to live quietly in

Switzerland with you and the boys." And in March, 1856, to his brother William: "I on the contrary half cannot half will not throw myself into it [his work] and feel the weight of it doubly in consequence. I am inclined to think it would have been the same with any active line of life on which I had found myself engaged." And in May, 1857, to his sister: "I have a positive thirst to see the Alps again, and two or three things I have in mind which I cannot finish till I have again breathed and smelt Swiss air." Two of these we have just seen, "The Terrace at Berne" and "Obermann Once More." One does not suppose that he brooded over Marguerite, or that on the other hand he kept the memory of her as a literary convenience. He still felt the retroaction of his crisis of 1849, still had to "slip his chain," and still thought of "all that *might* have been," and could not deny himself a longing backward look—as Orpheus to Marguerite's Eurydice.

III

There is certainly no need to exaggerate the claims of Marguerite on posterity. Her two principal poems and several lines and phrases from others constitute her immortality, and they are perhaps more than as a person she deserves. *Sic se res habent.* But her importance to Arnold is another matter and requires careful summary. Setting aside the two lighter pieces which Arnold finally removed to Early Poems, her seven poems present an almost plotted sequence: the troubled meeting in 1849, the trial parting in search of peace, the harsh farewell, the lyric interlude on a theme of isolation, and the oddly named "Absence" which confesses his unwilling renunciation—and also, perhaps, serves as transition to another love which ended in marriage. And then the long coda wherein Arnold explains that he is done with her, ten years after. Now, however much he may have dramatized himself and her, the note of actuality, the amount of circumstantial detail, and the air of verisimilitude are unmistakable, are in fact clearer than in "Faded Leaves," which is known to be biographical. We can hardly err therefore in giving them general, although not literal, credence. Or if the family tradition, as represented by his daughter Lady Sandhurst, is to be accepted: "that Arnold always insisted 'Marguerite' was imaginary," she was a work of the creative imagination which is often truer than bare truth. Yet it is hard to believe that the verses which too often have an air of impromptu, of spontaneous overflow, or outburst, of immediate feeling, and are some of them so rough as to betray the disorder of untranquil emotion—the two isolation poems always excepted—sprang from imagination alone. Nowhere else did Arnold show that kind of imagination. But what could he say, if pressed directly? or in what tone, with what inflection, did he say "imaginary"? Useless questions, for however the elementary details were embroidered for poetical ends, there was a Marguerite with whom he rehearsed a part and from whom he learned that it was no part for him to play.

Arnold might have said of "Switzerland" what Meredith said of "Modern Love": "A writer's verse is one of his methods of relieving himself of the burden within him"; and he might have quoted—

> We are betrayed by what is false within.

There are those who set a high value on passionate feeling and its transcendent power to exalt and even ennoble; there are those who envy the few who are capable of this intense emotion and unselfish absorption, for in its denial of the world and social obligations it has some kinship with religious ecstasy; but there are also those who set a higher value on their moral integrity and the strength of will and intellect, who cannot bear to surrender this integrity to the mere feelings, who (having learned from the moth) desire the flame only provided it is hard and gemlike and so are neither for Jehovah nor for his enemies. Arnold was one of these last. At his youthful crisis, which came rather late—for he was, at twenty-seven, still the "worldling," at least in the eyes of his family, and he had settled down only to the extent of becoming secretary to Lord Lansdowne two years before—he was perplexed by the choice between the world and solitude. In the sonnet he praised Shakespeare's aloofness from mortal affairs; in "Resignation" he extolled the ideal poet's detachment from mundane entanglements; his Empedocles plunged into the crater because in freeing himself from the world he could not escape from "thought," could not live in the light of his own soul—the dilemma from both sides; his Mycerinus withdrew in scorn from the world and its unjust gods to "the silence of the groves" and "the tumult of the feast"—and again Arnold betrayed his uncertainty by hinting that the king held aloof from the revelry and so

> Was calm'd, ennobled, comforted, sustain'd.

What course was *he* to choose? Poetry, the life contemplative, in the light of his own soul, in peace, away from "the raving world"? or that very world,

> the ungenial earth,
> Man's work-place,

with its promises and satisfactions? Well, he separated himself, as he put it, from Obermann (solitude and contemplation) and he renounced Marguerite (poetry and passion) at the same time. They had for him the reality of symbols; and it was Marguerite's rôle and opportunity to teach him—"We know beforehand all they can teach us: yet we are obliged to learn it directly from them"—that the heroic quality which holds the world well lost was not his. Perhaps she was right, whatever else. But he was never quite convinced. One should ponder his words in a letter to Clough as early as 1 May, 1853: "I feel immensely—and more clearly—what I have (I believe) lost and choked by my treatment of myself"; and one should read in the light of these words both "The Terrace at Berne" and "Obermann Once More," and that strange *poème de noces* "Stanzas from the Grande Chartreuse," together with many other phrasings in verse and prose: his dissatisfaction with the choice. When he writes

>And Marguerite I shall see no more

and brings Obermann on preaching Victorian progress, it is not so much that he mourns her loss or denies Senancourt's philosophy, as that he mourns his own loss and would return to Senancourt's solitude, slipping his chain. Perhaps the choice was right, for him; but he was still unreconciled. What we mourn, however, is that in the test of character (that modern shibboleth) Marguerite was not the woman to save him for poetry, and to save him from a life of school inspecting and journalistic controversies.

NOTE ON THE REARRANGEMENTS OF THE POEMS

In the 1849 volume, *The Strayed Reveller and Other Poems, By A.*, only one of the Marguerite poems appeared: "To My Friends, Who Ridiculed a Tender Leave-Taking," later renamed "A Memory Picture."

The next volume, *Empedocles on Etna, and Other Poems*, 1852, contained, after the title poem:

"The River"	(in 1855 "Faded Leaves i")
"Excuse"	(in 1869 "Urania")
"Indifference"	(in 1869 "Euphrosyne")
"Too Late"	(in 1855 "Faded Leaves ii")
"On the Rhine"	(in 1855 "Faded Leaves iv")
"Longing"	(in 1855 "Faded Leaves v")
"The Lake"	(in 1853 "Switzerland ii")
"Parting"	(in 1853 "Switzerland iv")
"Absence"	(in 1853 "Switzerland vi")
"Destiny"	(not reprinted by Arnold)
"To Marguerite" ["Yes, in the sea"]	(in 1853 "Switzerland v")

After ten more titles, including "Tristram and Iseult," appeared "A Farewell," which in 1854 became "Switzerland v." This early arrangement of some "Faded Leaves" poems and some "Switzerland" poems consecutively is to be noted.

In the next year, 1853, Arnold published, under his full name, *Poems. A New Edition* (later called *Poems. First Series*); it was a selection from the two preceding volumes, with eight new poems. Here the "Switzerland" group was first set up:

      i. "To My Friends"
     ii. "The Lake"
    iii. "A Dream"
    iv. "Parting"
     v. "To Marguerite"
    vi. "Absence"

The poems which here precede and follow are unrelated to either the "Switzerland" or the "Faded Leaves" group. There were no "Faded Leaves" poems in this volume. In 1854 a new edition was issued, containing of course no "Faded Leaves" poems, but with one change in the "Switzerland" group, namely "A Farewell" (which was not in the 1853 volume) was brought from its previous isolated position in the 1852 volume and became "Switzerland v"—the v and vi of 1853 now becoming vi and vii.

In the following year, 1855, appeared *Poems. Second Series*, a selection from the volumes of 1849 and 1852, but reprinting nothing from the 1853 and 1854 volumes. Here first the "Faded Leaves" group was set up:

      i. "The River"
     ii. "Too Late"
    iii. "Separation"
    iv. "On the Rhine"
     v. "Longing"

These were followed by "Self-Deception," then "Excuse" and "Indifference" (which in 1852 had stood between "The River" and "Too Late" as though they belonged together) and "Resignation," etc.

Two years later, in 1857, appeared the Third Edition of the 1853 volume. It also of course contained no "Faded Leaves" poems; but it added one new "Switzerland" poem, "We were apart..." entitled "To Marguerite."

Arnold's next volume of poems (except *Merope*, 1858) came ten years later: *New Poems*, 1867. It contained two new poems of interest here, "Calais Sands" and "The Terrace at Berne." "Dover Beach," which was also new, stood just between. In 1868 there was a second edition of this volume.

In 1869 appeared the so-called First Collected Edition, vol. i of which contained the "Faded Leaves" group from 1855, and vol. ii the "Switzerland" group, as in 1857 (except for the omission of "A Dream"), followed immediately by "Urania" (which had previously been called "Excuse"), "Euphrosyne" (which had previously been called "Indifference"), "Calais Sands," "Dover Beach," etc. Here it is to be noted that the two poems which under their first titles, "Excuse" and "Indifference," had in 1852 stood between two poems which later became i and ii of "Faded Leaves," and which in 1855 had followed the "Faded Leaves" group with only one intervening poem ("Self-Deception"), are now, in 1869, completely separated from their former associates and placed in a different volume; yet though they follow immediately the "Switzerland" group they precede "Calais Sands," which is certified to Mrs. Arnold. In 1877 the *Poems*, a "New and Complete Edition," were again issued in two volumes; followed by a new edition of the same, in 1881, with one change of interest here, the restoration of "A Dream."

In the meantime Arnold had published his *Selected Poems*, 1878, which was frequently reprinted. Here a section called Early Poems was created, to which was relegated the former "Switzerland i," *i.e.*, "To My Friends," now renamed "A Memory Picture." The "Switzerland" group now has taken its final form:

    i. "Meeting" ("The Lake," 1852, 1853, 1854, 1857, 1869)
   ii. "Parting" (1852, 1853, 1854, 1857, 1869)

iii. "A Farewell" (1852, 1854, 1857, 1869)
iv. "Isolation. To Marguerite" ["We were apart"] (1857, 1869)
v. "To Marguerite. Continued" ["Yes! in the sea"] (1852, 1853, 1854, 1857, 1869)
vi. "Absence" (1852, 1853, 1854, 1857, 1869)
vii. "The Terrace at Berne" (1867, 1869)

These poems were followed by "The Strayed Reveller," two excerpts from "Empedocles," "Urania," "Euphrosyne," "Calais Sands," "Dover Beach," etc. There were no "Faded Leaves" poems in the *Selected Poems*.

Finally, in 1885, appeared the Library Edition in three volumes (followed in 1890 by the posthumous *Poetical Works* in one volume) where for the first time since 1852, when the two groups were still unnamed and unseparated, the "Switzerland" and the "Faded Leaves" poems coexisted between the same covers. Vol. i contains Early Poems, Narrative Poems and Sonnets—among them "A Memory Picture," formally connected with the "Switzerland" group by Arnold's note to "Meeting," and followed by "A Dream." Vol. ii contains the Lyric and Elegiac Poems, and begins with the seven poems of the "Switzerland" group, and after five intervening titles come "Urania," "Euphrosyne," "Calais Sands," "Faded Leaves" (which had not been reprinted since 1869), "Despondency," "Self-Deception," "Dover Beach," etc.

Two generalizations may be reasonably drawn. One is the definite limitation of the Marguerite canon so far as Arnold wished it to be recognized. Of the nine poems, all but two bear her name either in the title or in the text; and of those two "Absence" was with the "Switzerland" poems in their first untitled arrangement and thereafter always included in the group. The other, "A Farewell," was distinctly separated from the group in 1852, was omitted in 1853, and thereafter always included. One may infer therefore that Arnold did not at first want it associated with Marguerite, but once he decided there was no hesitation. (The possibility that it was not written about her in the first instance, but added to her poems because of its similar content, need not be considered.) If any other poems were written for her or about her, Arnold has left no hint; and since he was so definite about the nine, criticism and speculation should be correspondingly cautious. Some have thought they saw her in "The Voice"; for a long time she was supposed to be in "Faded Leaves"; there is a Margaret in "The Forsaken Merman"; there are blue eyes in "Tristram and Iseult." But all such attempted extensions of the canon are risky and gratuitous. I, for one, however, should like to include "Destiny," both because it was among the Marguerite poems in 1852 and if Arnold had chosen to reprint it might well have remained among them, and also because its tone and meaning are consistent with them. For the rest, though the shifting positions are complicated in the explaining they show no sign of intentional concealment or (*pace* Professor Garrod) mystification. It has even been argued that "Arnold's frequent reconsideration of the content and order of the series suggests that references to Marguerite may be found elsewhere than in the 'Switzerland' group"; but reconsideration of the *order* of the series, which was frequent enough, need not be confused with reconsideration of the *content*. And such a remark as "I think I find her even in unlikely contexts" hardly commends itself to serious criticism. Arnold seems to have hesitated for a time about "A Farewell" and he could not easily make up his mind about the position of "A Memory Picture" and "A Dream," probably because of their lighter tone. But this is all.

The other conclusion is that Arnold clearly meant, after 1852, to keep the "Switzerland" and "Faded Leaves" poems apart. The former were always in his *First Series* and the latter in his *Second Series,* until the Collected Edition of 1869, and then they were in different volumes. He excluded "Faded Leaves" from the *Selected Poems.* We know now that the "Faded Leaves" poems were written to Miss Wightman and represent the early stages of his wooing of the *"unerreichbare schöne,"* and there is no point in canvassing the reasons, never plausible though characteristic of much Arnold criticism, why they ever were confused with the Marguerite poems. Within this group, however, is a point worth a moment's attention. In 1852 "Excuse" ("Urania") and "Indifference" ("Euphrosyne") stood within the poems which in 1855 became "Faded Leaves"; but in 1855 they followed "Faded Leaves" with one intervening poem ("Self-Deception"). In 1869 they followed "The Terrace at Berne" though they could not properly be read as related to it, and immediately preceded "Calais Sands," which was written for Miss Wightman, and "Dover Beach," which is usually associated with her. In 1878 (*Selected Poems*) there were three poems between them and "The Terrace at Berne," but they still immediately preceded "Calais Sands" and "Dover Beach"; and this volume did not contain "Faded Leaves." In 1885 there were five poems between them and "The Terrace at Berne" and then the (final) order became: "Urania," "Euphrosyne," "Calais Sands," "Faded Leaves," "Despondency," "Self-Deception," "Dover Beach." The increasing separation between the last of the "Switzerland" group and these two is probably not significant, but it does seem significant that when they were first printed they were surrounded by "Faded Leaves" poems, next were separated only by "Self-Deception," and thereafter stood always just before "Calais Sands." Whatever else may be implied, I am inclined to believe that they were written about Miss Wightman.

Finally, it appears that these rearrangements afford no evidence for dating the composition of any of the poems beyond the obvious terminus ad quem of the date of publication.

PAULL FRANKLIN BAUM

Duke University

V
Carlyle and T. H. Huxley

KICKED INTO THE world a boy without guide or training, or with worse than none, I confess to my shame that few men have drunk deeper of all kinds of sin than I. Happily, my course was arrested in time . . . and for long years I have been slowly and painfully climbing . . . towards better things. And when I look back, what do I find to have been the agents of my redemption? The hope of immortality or of future reward? I can honestly say that for these fourteen years such a consideration has not entered my head. No, I can tell you exactly what has been at work. *Sartor Resartus* led me to know that a deep sense of religion was compatible with the entire absence of theology. Secondly, science and her methods gave me a resting-place independent of authority and tradition. Thirdly, love opened up to me a view of the sanctity of human nature, and impressed me with a deep sense of responsibility.[1]

Huxley wrote these words on September 23, 1860. His four-year-old son, then an only child, had died but a few days before. The tragedy had occasioned an epistolary exchange of peculiar significance, for the bereaved father was already a notorious "agnostic" and his correspondent was the churchman Charles Kingsley, who, though a complete stranger, had with characteristic courage written a letter of sympathy. Huxley's reply is at once a personal confession and a statement of faith. As he was a man of much less than average turpitude, the confession is not to be taken very seriously. It is probably the at-

[1] Leonard Huxley, *Life and Letters of Thomas Henry Huxley* (New York, 1900), I, 237.

tempt of a deeply moral nature, frantic with grief, to explain his loss according to some sort of moral justice. The statement of faith which closes the paragraph is interesting chiefly because of the basic importance assigned to the influence of Carlyle.

Perhaps too little has been made of Huxley's loss of faith. Certainly, the warfare between Huxley and religion was essentially fratricidal. By temperament and destiny he was a cleric who began as a partial non-conformist and ended as very nearly a complete one. By nature he was a superb teacher who deeply reverenced his profession in youth and in maturity exercised it from nearly every platform but the pulpit. As a child he admired Sir Herbert Oakley, the local rector. Once—if the event is of any significance—he turned his pinafore around backwards to represent a surplice, and delivered a sermon in the manner of his hero to the maids in the kitchen.[2] A few years later, listening to another clergyman, he heard "dark allusions to 'sceptics' and 'infidels,' " and "from the horror of the tone in which they were mentioned," wondered whether they "belonged to the criminal classes."[3] Soon afterwards he began that course of amazingly rapid desultory reading, which, growing always more intensive and systematic and continuing throughout life, made him one of the most learned, and the least Anglican, of Victorians. He had a boy's eye for big titles, from Hutton's *Theory of the Earth* to Sir William Hamilton's "Philosophy of the Unconditioned"; nor was his eye bigger than his stomach. And as knowledge increased, reverence dwindled. He noticed that village parsons frequently used bad grammar, and used it to little purpose, except to reveal ignorance and prejudice. It was Hamilton's article, which he found in an old volume of *The Edinburgh*,[4] that finally explained everything, and released him from any further need to take parsons seriously. Sir William ponder-

[2] Thomas Henry Huxley, "Autobiography," *Methods and Results* (New York, 1896), p. 5.
[3] Thomas Henry Huxley, "Prologue," *Science and Christian Tradition* (New York, 1896), p. 21.
[4] A review of M. V. Cousin's *Cours de Philosophie*, L (1829), 194-221.

ously undermines all conditioned and finite knowledge in order to establish the Scottish Kirk in the transcendental sublimity of the unconditioned. Huxley abandoned the Kirk, but embraced the scepticism. At the age of fifteen he found, probably with some complacency, that he had developed the opinions of the criminal classes.

But if he felt very clever, he must also have felt rather lonely in those opinions. It is not easy to be sceptical when most people believe. Moreover, he was not, like so many nowadays, comfortably accustomed to a universe locked up in transience and death. As a child he had known a Creation with a window looking up to a Creator and a door opening out on immortality. He could not have seen the door and the window closed without some bitterness and fear. He never suggests that agnosticism is a cheerful creed, and he refers with some contempt to clergymen who help themselves over the problem of life with the sleeping pill, or "anesthetic," of a conventional faith.[5] As late as 1847, in the first year of his long cruise in the *Rattlesnake*, he wrote:

"Ich kann nichts anders! Gott hilfe mir!" Morals and religion are one wild whirl to me—of them the less said the better. In the region of the intellect alone can I find free and innocent play for such faculties as I possess. And it is well for me that my way of life allows me to get rid of the "malady of thought" in a course of action so suitable to my tastes, as that laid open to me by this voyage.

And in 1849 he adds, beside the same entry: "Is it better with me now? A little."[6]

This passage suggests that he took comfort in Carlyle's doctrine of work. In any case, what prevented his religious problem from ever coming to an acute crisis was probably devotion to Carlyle, who was the chief hero of his youthful reading. Unfortunately, his statements of indebtedness are nearly as vague as they are

[5] "The Evolution of Theology: An Anthropological Study," *Science and Hebrew Tradition* (New York, 1897), p. 287.
[6] Julian Huxley, ed., *T. H. Huxley's Diary of the Voyage of H.M.S. Rattlesnake* (London, 1935), p. 38.

emphatic. He gives evidence of having read *Sartor Resartus, Past and Present*, the *Latter-Day Pamphlets*, and "Characteristics," as well as others of the *Critical and Miscellaneous Essays*. One gathers that he gained from Carlyle sympathy for the poor, a hatred of shams, devotion to work, the impetus to study German language and literature, and—as the letter to Kingsley acknowledges—a deep sense of religion divorced from theology.[7] In spite of the evidence, one may well ask, what could a cool, clear-headed rationalist like Huxley see in a hot, steamy-headed moralist like Carlyle? The answer is that Huxley was not always so cool and clear-headed as he seemed; that when he read Carlyle he was very young, with some of a young man's romanticism; and that he was also a Victorian, with all a Victorian's earnestness.

Carlyle's vast contemporary fame depended on the moral and literary grandeur with which he invested ambiguous answers to contemporary dilemmas. Of the religious dilemma Huxley had been painfully aware, and probably very much in Carlyle's terms. For if he found virtue in Carlyle's cure, he must have suffered from Carlyle's disease. If he embraced Carlyle's stentorian moralism, half naturalistic, half Calvinistic, so fervently that its effects are traceable in his whole later career, he must at one time or another have received dark intimations of the "Everlasting No." Again, he had marked literary sensitivity. If his hero could not provide logical answers, at least he provided poetical ones. Finally, Huxley was the kind of man who, if he did not need theological certainty, undoubtedly craved ethical direction and significance in his life. He had a moralist's conscientiousness without a moralist's gift for introspection. He either dreaded or did not care or was unable to look inward. For such a man, Carlyle's crude apotheosis of action, with its convenient sacrifice of ultimate and interior knowledge to efficiency and service, must have seemed at once a justification and the answer to a spiritual need.

[7] L. Huxley, *Life and Letters*, I, 9, 10, 16, 237; II, 285; Leonard Huxley, "Carlyle and Huxley: Early Influences," *The Cornhill Magazine*, LXXI (1932), 290-302.

What the two men had in common was, fundamentally, the search for truth; and since the older man's achievement was in large degree the younger man's inspiration, it might be well to recall Carlyle's own early development. Like Huxley, he passed from orthodoxy to scepticism. Logic, matter, and David Hume made him an infidel. To a mind like Carlyle's doubt was loathsome, not simply because he infinitely preferred a live universe to a dead one and an heroic one to a mechanical, but because he preferred strength to weakness.[8] He felt that he was a prophet able to instruct mankind. Doubt meant division, humiliation, paralysis. Or, more accurately, the tragedy was intensely personal. Having dramatically proclaimed in the person of Teufelsdröckh that he would die for cosmic truth, Carlyle shifts almost at once to "Alas! the fearful Unbelief is unbelief in yourself."[9] Not to know God was not to have an intelligible theater in which to develop one's potentialities. It is not surprising that he invented a universe to set off his own talents, fashioning it in the image of his ambitions, tastes, tradition, and —one is tempted to say—his indigestion. The subjectivity of the German idealists provided him with an instrument and a framework. He decided that matter was "but an air-image," "the reflex of our own inward Force;"[10] and logic, which he now hated as a disease, but the instrument of the understanding, of a lower, earthly kind of reason. The higher reason was intuition, direct insight into the mind of God through the transparent "air-images" which were the world of man and nature. His treatment of this faculty is confused. Sometimes his intuition is ethical and Calvinistic, exalting moral law in God and man, and enjoining reverence and obedience. Sometimes it is romantic and expansive, exalting force and dynamic spontaneity, and enjoining the virtues of wonder and intensity. Yet whatever it is,

[8] *Sartor Resartus, Carlyle's Works,* Édition de Luxe (Boston, 1884), I, 125. When a volume number is given after a Carlyle title, it will be understood that this edition is referred to.
[9] *Ibid.,* I, 126.
[10] *Ibid.,* I, 42.

Carlyle's intuition is always aesthetic and in a curious pragmatic way realistic. Since every fact is fundamentally symbolic, its meaning depends on an effort of the individual imagination and its validity on passionate expression or effectual action. Since the whole world is fundamentally symbolic, its precise, literal meaning becomes less important; so that, as potential knowledge, it is only secondarily a museum for investigation and primarily a battle ground of imaginative subjectivities, where poetry proposes and will disposes. History is the unfolding of divine ideas in the lives of great men, of which there are two kinds—poets who persuade and strong men who act. They are the intermediaries between dream and reality, thought and deed. Truth is not so much discovered, as conceived and made. It is poetry that prevails in practical life. In the long run, it is what vividly survives, as action or idea, in the vast competition which is history.

These ideas seem very far from the smooth agnosticism of Huxley, in whom matter, logic, and David Hume eventually did their worst.[11] And yet the difference between Hume and Huxley might, in large degree, be summed up as the influence of Carlyle.

As a boy in his 'teens, Huxley seems to have accepted such works as "Characteristics" and *Sartor Resartus* with little reservation. Negatively, they confirmed him in his agnosticism, leading him to reject revelation and all divine metaphysics in the old dogmatic sense.[12] Positively, they provided him with a belief which probably softened the impact of scepticism and taught him that "a deep sense of religion was compatible with the entire absence of theology." What this sense of religion involves one may guess from his enthusiasm for the German essays, among which the "Novalis" contains a lengthy discussion of Kantian and post-Kantian idealism. A quotation from "Characteristics," copied down in his journal at the age of seventeen, betrays him

[11] See Huxley's *Hume, With Helps to the Study of Berkeley* (New York, 1897).
[12] "Characteristics," XIV, 365-69; *Sartor Resartus*, I, 146-47.

even into a minor heresy against science: "The healthy understanding, we should say, is neither the argumentative nor the Logical, but the Intuitive, for the end of the understanding is not to prove and find reasons but to know and believe."[13]

Probably Carlyle also awakened the young man's literary sense. One is tempted to ask why he did no more, why he did not turn so fine a literary talent permanently to literature. As a matter of fact, he did not even stimulate it to temporary action. For Huxley, writing was always an instrument. It meant the art of clarity, the art of controversy, which, particularly in later years, he cultivated as a virtuoso, but always for the purposes of the scientist and the social critic. Literature in the narrow sense could hardly have claimed him, partly because he was too practical and utilitarian to care for mere art and partly because he was not sufficiently interested in its characteristic subject matter, which is man as such. He could become absorbed in man as a physical mechanism, as an anthropoid ape, as a citizen and social animal, as a delicate machine for the discovery of scientific truth; but not in man as a personality and a human being. With all his splendid talents for friendship and affection, he remained, from the deeper psychological point of view, indifferent to people. In fact, as I have indicated, he was not even interested in himself. Seldom has so vivid and articulate a writer had so little of importance to say, even in his most intimate letters, about himself.

A few months after foreswearing logic and evidence in the idiom of "Characteristics," Huxley embraced them with a fanaticism that increased with increasing years. He was converted to science by the eminent anatomist and physiologist Wharton Jones, under whose influence he came in his first term as a medical student at Charing Cross Hospital. From Jones he learned exact, painstaking scientific method in the search for truth. His sense of discipline had found its most typical expression.

[13] L. Huxley, *Life and Letters*, I, 14.

Huxley, like Carlyle, had an imperative personal need for certainty, for in him the will to achieve and dominate was perhaps equally strong, though less self-conscious and dramatic. He was also magnificently endowed for the life of action. Swiftness and clarity of thought, as he himself observes,[14] were the essential qualities of his mind; and he had all the coolness, the sureness, and the self-confidence which accompany them. He was always mobilized for action. He never hesitated, was never less than himself. He was a rapid and voluminous reader, a ready and eloquent speaker, a facile and brilliant writer. In short, he possessed the obvious virtues in nearly as much splendor as Macaulay. Sir Mountstuart Grant Duff correctly remarked that he might have been one of the most successful politicians of his age[15]—and perhaps he was. But like all strong men conscious of their strength and eager to exert it, he needed a rock, "a resting place,"[16] from which to spring. This he found in science.

Both Carlyle and Huxley had begun by recognizing the difference between final and contingent knowledge. Both had set up truth as the key to life, but whereas Carlyle's truth was poetic and pragmatic, Huxley's was scientific and verifiable. They emphasized alternate instruments of the Kantian system. Carlyle chose *Vernunft*, and regarded the world as a luminous symbol of Eternity. Huxley chose *Verstand*, and regarded the world as likely to be very solid and opaque. Carlyle attempted to discredit the understanding by emphasizing its limitations.[17] Huxley rested in those limitations with a truly heroic firmness. He attained his heaven by denying it.

And in this denial there is a Puritan rigor which must have been encouraged by the reading of Carlyle. He turned science and the agnosticism which is its philosophical equivalent into a principle of self-abnegation, extracting from the very sternness of scientific method and the very nullity of scientific pre-

---
[14] "Autobiography," *Methods and Results*, p. 4.
[15] L. Huxley, *Life and Letters*, I, 381.
[16] See the quotation that opens this article.
[17] *Sartor Resartus*, I, 28, 40-42, 193-95.

tensions to spiritual knowledge, a measure of spiritual consolation. As an agnostic he professed no opinions on ultimate questions. Nevertheless, he was inclined to disbelieve in immortality because it was an idea flattering to human wishes.[18] Particularly when pressed in controversy, he willingly enlarged on the uncertainty of knowledge. The laws of nature might suddenly be abrogated, or nature itself, as we know it through the senses, might be a phantasm, having no relation to any genuine reality. In his scientific work, whether of teaching or research, he was a fanatic of method, submitting not only his own results but even the hallowed platitudes of textbooks to careful testing.[19] For him, science embodied a Calvinistic imperative. Had Carlyle been a scientist, he would probably have been such a scientist as Huxley.

Apparently Huxley felt that science exerts spiritual force in three ways, all more or less related: it imposes a discipline of accuracy and fairmindedness; it provides a knowledge of nature; and it frees the mind from prejudice and superstition. He nowhere asserts that intellectual discipline naturally becomes moral discipline, but he does say that science is truth-telling and that truth-telling is the basis of all the virtues.[20] Science is not only organized common sense but organized honesty. Does not its immense success offer the spectacle of a poetic justice which may eventually regenerate mankind? But with all his confidence in science as discipline, Huxley seems to have expected more from an increased knowledge of nature. "Learn what is true," he wrote of such knowledge, "in order to do what is right."[21] To know nature is probably an aid to virtue, but to know man and society is certainly a much greater aid. This introduces the question of what Huxley meant by *nature*.

[18] John Fiske, "Reminiscences of Huxley," *Annual Report of the Board of Regents of the Smithsonian Institute*, 1900, p. 720.
[19] L. Huxley, *Life and Letters*, I, 254-55.
[20] Leonard Huxley, "Home Memories," *Nature*, CXV (1925), 699.
[21] William K. Brooks, *Annual Report of the Board of Regents of the Smithsonian Institution*, 1900, p. 705.

Late in life a careful reading of Rousseau showed him the dangers of deducing an ethical system from the natural order. In such essays as "Natural and Political Rights" (1890) and "Evolution and Ethics" (1893) he makes a clear distinction between nature and human society, the law for brute and the law for man. Up until 1890, however, he regarded man simply as a part of nature, into which, under the influence of Carlyle and probably of Wordsworth, he read important moral and aesthetic values. If nature is beautiful, obviously it is an enoblement of the mind, and therefore a moral help, to study her. If she is moral, she becomes, quite simply, a peculiarly long and complicated treatise on morals. To study her is to become learned in virtue.

So far as Huxley's own career is concerned, the beauty of nature must have been an inspiration not only to good conduct but to scientific study. Books like *Sartor Resartus*, merely as nature poetry, must have given an aesthetic impetus to the biological investigations pursued on the *Rattlesnake* and to the geological observations carried on with Tyndall in the Alps. But books like *Sartor* and *Past and Present* were probably even more influential in determining his ideas about nature as a moral and spiritual entity. In many respects, his attitude closely parallels that of Carlyle. There is the same tendency to see God in nature, the same tendency to merge ethical and natural law. In the famous letter to Kingsley, for example, he refers in so many words to the "Divine Government" as embodied in nature and the system of things, and declares that it is "wholly just." "As we live we are paid for living."[22] But perhaps what is written in the extremity of grief should not be taken too exactly. The great bulk of Huxley's writings indicates that he was not a theist. It also indicates, however, that, with all his scrupulous detachment, he was not sufficiently self-critical to be altogether consistent. He steadily maintained that, whereas religion was

[22] L. Huxley, *Life and Letters*, I, 236. See also T. H. Huxley, *Scientific Memoirs*, Michael Foster and E. Ray Lankester, eds. (London, 1891), I, 307, 311.

anthropomorphic, science was entirely impersonal; yet high and solid as he built the walls of his impersonality, he was constantly smuggling God into his citadel in a metaphor. For example, the famous metaphor of the hidden chess player concludes:

> The chess-board is the world, the pieces are the phenomena of the universe, the rules of the game are what we call the laws of Nature. The player on the other side is hidden from us. We know that his play is always fair, just and patient. But also we know, to our cost, that he never overlooks a mistake, or makes the smallest allowance for ignorance. To the man who plays well, the highest stakes are paid, with that sort of overflowing generosity with which the strong shows delight in strength. And one who plays ill is checkmated—without haste, but without remorse.[23]

Here science is very close to anthropomorphism. The passage is not easy to interpret, but the general sense seems to be that if you know the laws of nature and play the game well and strongly, you will obtain justice. To the soured modern reader this may seem nothing but a very sweet, Victorian way of saying that in nature the law of strength and cunning prevails. I am inclined to think, however, that Huxley did not know quite what he meant. In the poetic overtones of the passage there is a distinct suggestion that justice inheres in the physical order. Huxley's words are strikingly similar to those describing nature as a sphinx in *Past and Present*.[24]

Almost as much quoted, and perhaps even more interesting, is another pronouncement on nature from the Kingsley letter:

> Sit down before fact as a little child, be prepared to give up every preconceived notion, follow humbly wherever and to whatever abysses nature may lead, or you shall learn nothing. I have only begun to find content and peace of mind since I have resolved at all risks to do this.[25]

[23] "A Liberal Education; and Where to Find It," *Science and Education* (New York, 1897), p. 82.
[24] *Past and Present*, XII, 8-9.
[25] L. Huxley, *Life and Letters*, I, 235.

But to sit down before fact as a little child, with humility, trust, and reverence, is perhaps to read something into fact. It is to sense the infinite in the finite, the boundless mystery in the little flower in the crannied wall. Apparently, matter does not need to be dialectically exorcised to become transparent. Here Huxley's facts threaten to become as insubstantial and infinitely suggestive as Carlyle's symbols. The passage expresses spiritual detachment, but not quite scientific impersonality. Its implications are not necessarily anthropomorphic, but they tend to be spiritual and other-worldly. Here Huxley apprehends fact with *Vernunft* as well as *Verstand*.

And yet he steadily refused to see the consequences of his attitude. Why? The question takes us back to the Victorian dilemma, which was critical for both Huxley and Carlyle. A brave new world of thought and action was rapidly unfolding which, as it revealed more and more glittering possibilities, came into even more drastic contradiction with traditional ethics and religion. The new world had no ultimate spiritual rationale. The old ethics and religion had no practical content. Most Victorians solved the problem by keeping very busy and allowing contradictions to creep back into the dictionary. Carlyle elaborated this procedure into a moral doctrine: "Work, and a real, intelligible universe will grow up around you." While Carlyle's doctrine of work was undoubtedly an inspiration to Huxley, inevitably it meant somewhat different things to men so different.

It might (rather extravagantly) be argued that the greatest influences on Carlyle were Hume and Gibbon: they contributed so much to make him what they were not. Certainly their neat logical scepticism was the focus which projected the contradictions of the age into his mind with a persistent, gnawing sharpness, producing at length a general inward conflict in which intellectual vanity was at war with worldly ambition, personal integrity with duty to parents, logic with common sense, and reason with spiritual inclination.[26] It is no wonder that thereafter logic gave him indigestion and self-inquiry seemed to him a disease. His doctrine of work suffers the consequences. It is at once the most imposing and heroic formulation of the Victorian faith in process, and a curious conglomerate of Scottish peasant industriousness, utilitarian optimism, artistic self-consciousness, romantic rainbow-questing, and Christian meditation without inwardness. It declares all labor sacred with little regard to kind or to the end envisaged. On the analogy of the potter's wheel, it asserts that movement creates its own adequate stability and control, that environment and especially the laws of nature provide a sufficient moral discipline. It proclaims a faith in man's future without offering any coherent theory either of man or the future. Here it is closely related to the ambiguities in Carlyle's picture of history, which suggests a cyclical morality drama in which God, while inculcating the broad, rough principles of justice, strains rather self-consciously for artistic effect. All that partakes of the infinite is divine. As historical symbols are divine in their infinite, indefinite suggestiveness, so all human effort is divine in its infinite possibility. The splendid picture of Columbus sailing into the vastness of the western ocean appropriately culminates Carlyle's most elaborate treatment of the subject of labor.[27] At its best, his doctrine represents great moral courage with great moral blindness. At its worst, it suggests a reluctance to define for fear the definition may not be titanic enough.

Other than to acknowledge indebtedness to Carlyle, Huxley nowhere attempts any formulation of his ideas on this subject, yet his faith in process, in activity as such, is striking. As a personal resource, work was for him, as for Carlyle, a means of gratifying ambition, satisfying a sense of duty, and escaping from inward contradictions. As a doctrine, it represents one thing—

[26] David A. Wilson, *Carlyle Till Marriage* (London, 1923), pp. 78-79, 109-11, 145-49, 248-52.
[27] "Labour" in *Past and Present*.

faith in the future of science. To work at science was to work for the certainty of almost unlimited human knowledge and power.[28] By discovering the laws of social organization, science will answer the questions of Carlyle's sphinx and eventually solve the problem of poverty itself.[29] By revealing the laws of nature and by thus enabling man to place himself, in Carlyle's sense, more closely under natural discipline, it will improve human virtue and make moral progress a reality. By pursuing matter to its ultimate intricacies in the nerve cells of the human brain, it will probably unlock the mysteries of spirit and throw light on the great problems of epistemology.[30] Though admitting there is no proof that matter is the key to reality, Huxley is a devoted materialist. His materialism is part of his optimism, even of his idealism. If matter is real, then indeed miracles become not impossible, but probable and almost certain.

Science will also continue to destroy sham, prejudice, superstition, and hypocrisy, achieving truth by the elimination of error. Acting on this conviction, Huxley entered on the Scriptural controversies which earned him his own epithet of *episcopophagus* and brought him his most characteristic fame. In the one explicit reference to Carlyle's emphasis on work, he says:

There is nothing of permanent value..., nothing that satisfies quiet reflection—except the sense of having worked according to one's capacity and light, to make things clear and get rid of cant and shams of all sorts. That was the lesson I learned from Carlyle's books when I was a boy, and it has stuck by me all my life.[31]

Carlyle's hatred of shams was not only puritan but romantic and primitivistic. They represented artificiality as opposed to nature, mechanism as opposed to spontaneity, shallow self-consciousness as opposed to the creative profundities of the un-

[28] "Six Lectures to Working Men 'On Our Knowledge of the Causes of the Phenomena of Organic Nature,'" *Darwiniana*, pp. 359-60.
[29] "Evolution and Ethics," *Evolution and Ethics* (New York, 1896), p. 218.
[30] "Prologue," *Science and Christian Tradition*, pp. 46-47.
[31] Letter to W. Platt Ball, Oct. 27, 1890, in L. Huxley, *Life and Letters*, II, 285.

conscious. Moreover, mechanical pretense inhibits the natural flow of creative reality. According to Carlyle's cyclical conception of history, the shams of a decadent age must be cleared away before the vitalism of a constructive one can assert itself.[32] Hence the usefulness of Humes and Voltaires, otherwise so contemptible:

Of our Modern Metaphysics, accordingly, may not this already be said, that if they have produced no Affirmation, they have destroyed much Negation? It is a disease expelling a disease: the fire of Doubt, as above hinted, consuming away the Doubtful; that so the Certain come to light, and again lie visible on the surface.[33]

The moral inspiration of Carlyle encouraged Huxley to continue the destructive work of Voltaire. He was not actuated by a cyclical or romantic theory of history. Rather, his negative attitude toward religion proceeded in large degree from the nature of his position. As the champion of science he was necessarily the hostile critic of revelation. He had to attack the Pentateuch because it contradicted the discoveries of Lyell and Darwin. He had to wage war on demons and miracles because they contradicted the principle of the uniformity of nature, on which all science is founded. He discomfited bishops and archdeacons because their mode of argument was often hypocritical and unscientific. Yet his interests went beyond the mere exploding of superstition and prejudice. Thanking Edward Clodd for his *Jesus of Nazareth,* he wrote in 1879:

In spirit, matter, and form it appears to me to be exactly what people like myself have been wanting. For though for the last quarter of a century I have done all that lay in my power to oppose and destroy the idolatrous accretions of Judaism and Christianity, I have never had the slightest sympathy for those who, as the Germans say, would "throw the child away with the bath"—and when I was a member of the London School Board I fought for the retention of the Bible, to the great scandal of some of my Liberal friends.[34]

[32] Hill Shine, *Carlyle and the Saint-Simonians: The Concept of Historical Periodicity* (Baltimore, 1941), pp. 2, 19, 24, 25, 30-33 ff.
[33] "Characteristics," XIV, 381.
[34] L. Huxley, *Life and Letters,* II, 9.

What Huxley wanted to preserve was the best moral teaching of the Bible. In his "Evolution of Theology,"[35] he explores the field of comparative religion at some length to show that the higher the religion, the more ethics and the less dogma and ceremony.

But when every allowance has been made for the nature of his position and the breadth of his sympathies, it must be confessed that much of his writing, particularly on religion, is negative and critical in emphasis. Through many years of brilliant warfare against Noah's Ark and the Gadarene swine, he never once attempts to define either Jesus's teaching or its relation to modern life. Behind his scriptural controversies, as behind John Stuart Mill's defense of free speech in *Liberty,* lies the conception, which utilitarian argument so often implies yet so seldom expresses, that in the competition among opinions truth survives as an accumulating residue. "The struggle for existence," wrote Huxley of *The Origin of Species* after defending it triumphantly for twenty-one years, "holds as much in the intellectual as in the physical world. A theory is a species of thinking, and its right to exist is coextensive with its power of resisting extinction by its rivals."[36] Carlyle's "fire of Doubt . . . consuming away the Doubtful; that so the Certain come to light"[37] is very close to this idea, for it is obviously part of the broader idea, applied in so many fields of nineteenth-century thought, that competition produces excellence.

And so Huxley labored mightily at pumping off the gases of religious error in order that religious truth might eventually become visible as a tiny speck of near-certainty in a great vacuum of opinion. His justification was Carlyle's, minus the cyclical theory of history: He was preparing the ground for sounder beliefs—presumably for a religion with scientific ethics and no theology. Such a prospect is perfectly legitimate, except that

---

[35] *Science and Hebrew Tradition,* pp. 287-372.
[36] "The Coming of Age of 'The Origin of Species,'" *Darwiniana* (N.Y.: D. Appleton, 1897), p. 229.
[37] See p. 17.

Huxley pays too little attention to it. Sometimes he seems simply too much exhilarated by the pleasant excitement of window-smashing to think much about what to do with the empty spaces. Sometimes he seems positively unwilling to think about them. The Comtists, for example, who attempted to construct a scientific religion, draw some of his most deadly fire; and while no doubt they deserved it, still his sharpness is significant. Here again, Huxley is open to the accusation of believing rather blindly in process, of postponing his problems to the future. Basically, his fault—and that of many other Victorians, including Carlyle—is a reluctance to define. Carlyle was sufficiently constructive, but he avoided the final responsibilities of construction by an ambiguous use of words, particularly such words as *nature* and *intuition*. Huxley took refuge not only in ambiguities, but in the bright, reassuring clarity of negative criticism. As an agnostic he was prepared to define the magnitude of his ultimate ignorance, but not, as a moralist, to define any minimum of ultimate knowledge.

Few men [wrote Huxley shortly after Carlyle's death in 1881] can have dissented more strongly from his way of looking at things than I; but I should not yield to the most devoted of his followers in gratitude for the bracing wholesome influence of his writings when, as a very young man, I was essaying without rudder or compass to strike out a course for myself.[38]

In other words, Carlyle, though a moulding force upon Huxley's youth, was a diminishing one upon his maturer career. We must therefore not expect any close relationship between the ideas of these two men on educational, political, and social theory, with which Huxley was largely occupied in later years. Carlyle regarded society as an organism ruled by imagination, which expresses itself in various kinds of hero worship. Huxley regarded society as a body of individuals historically united by an implicit social contract and ruled ultimately by reason and expediency, which are ideally embodied in science. Nevertheless,

[38] Letter to Lord Stanley of Alderly, in L. Huxley, *Life and Letters*, II, 36-37.

early influences are persistent, and though he differed radically on fundamentals, Huxley may have owed certain broad convictions and tendencies, at least in part, to his early reading of Carlyle. These are, on the one hand, distrust of laissez-faire and of extreme democracy;[39] and, on the other, belief in the importance of genius[40] and of moral education.

Had he never read Carlyle, Huxley would probably have been less confused, less poetic, and considerably more utilitarian. What Carlyle chiefly contributed was not ideas but temperament. He developed the Victorian in Huxley. And in the Victorian age what could have been more important? He strengthened the moral fervor and the sense of discipline which gave to Huxley's strenuous advocacy of science an invaluable respectability at a time when science was confronted with the serried ranks of righteousness. Carlyle did not greatly change Huxley's mind, but he probably made it more influential.

[39] See "Administrative Nihilism," *Methods and Results*, pp. 251-89.
[40] *Ibid.*, p. 256.

WILLIAM IRVINE

Stanford University

VI

The Revolt from "Rationalism" in the Seventies and Some of its Literary Consequences

IN THE SPRING OF 1869 Tennyson assisted the journalist James Knowles in the founding of a Metaphysical Society for the free discussion of the old faith in its relations to the new science.[1] Whether or not, as one less reverent member suggested, the Laureate wished to "consult the experts" about the possibility of his having "such a thing as a soul,"[2] he most certainly hoped to discover the means by which the "advanced knowledge" of his time and the spiritual ends of man were to be reconciled. And a like impulse animated a number of the Metaphysicians of diverse creeds who met throughout the seventies for monthly debate. Among the orthodox or at least the theologically minded, Manning the Romanist, Hutton the Anglican, and James Martineau the impassioned Unitarian strove conscientiously to meet with respect the great argument of science. Ranged against them, Huxley the agnostic, Clifford the "free-thinker," Tyndall with his awe of nature, Harrison with his Religion of Humanity, all confessed to the need of some

[1] On the Society, see Alan Willard Brown, *The Metaphysical Society* (New York, 1947).
[2] See James Sully, *My Life and Friends* (London, 1918), p. 201.

moral code, an ethic to be rescued from the immoralities of ancient dogma. Few, however, achieved the compromise of Gladstone, who remained both conservative and radical; for few could match his strange "impartiality," his talent for "being furiously earnest on both sides of a question."[3] Each followed the logic of a differing mind with dutiful attention, only to return, perplexed but unshaken, to his own first premises of fact or faith. Thus from the long deliberation emerged no new synthesis. The final truce between science and religion, between the apostles of induction and the men of intuition, meant no final victory for either. It served only further to departmentalize human concerns and so to weaken the high Victorian assumption, once essential to every literary artist, that science and faith and art coalesced in one universal design, that, as Tennyson himself long ago had dreamed, mind and soul according well might make one music as before.

Defending the "scientific" method at a select Metaphysical symposium or on a public lecture platform or in the columns of the great liberal reviews, the "experts" of the new sciences— or rather that articulate group we may call the "rationalists" who championed scientific induction—were far from eager to give any poet such spiritual reassurance as would demand recourse to a discarded supernaturalism. Limiting themselves to the known and the knowable, they had behind them the tangible evidences of the laboratory, the apparent and immediate drama of empirical research. Content to forego the old certitude, they entered debate with buoyant self-assurance. To the free intelligence, they felt, the full truth would at last be freely revealed. Frederic Harrison accordingly could dismiss Christianity with its "pessimism as to the essential dignity of man" as a "degrading superstition,"[4] for which he might substitute his own more

[3] Houghton on Gladstone's "impartiality"; see Marquess of Crewe, "Lord Houghton," Harley Granville-Barker, ed., *The Eighteen-Seventies* (Cambridge, 1929), p. 10.

[4] Quoted by R. H. Hutton, *Contemporary Thought and Thinkers* (London, 1894), I, 300.

"rational" dogmas. And Huxley could rebuke all forms of "clericalism," as the chief impediment to free inquiry, "the deadly enemy of science" and so of all that was demonstrably true.[5] "Freethought" would destroy all false creeds and systems and then somehow, said Karl Pearson, would be in a position to accomplish its most solemn service, "the relief of spiritual misery"[6]—albeit the misery induced by the collapse of myth and ritual. For the only effectual advocates of any reform of benefit to man, wrote Harriet Martineau, were people who followed truth wherever it led.[7] And truth, as she conceived it, led inevitably away from the Unitarian theology of her brother James into the Positivist world of Auguste Comte—a bracing but rather bleak world where she could be stringently moral, though she might at times worry a little when she "thought of the pain which her new belief in personal annihilation would carry to the heart of some friends of hers who were widows."[8] Huxley, to be sure, came to question the possibility of grounding any ethic on the discoveries of natural science, even as he came to deplore the false analogies that the Spencerians had drawn between biological and social evolution. Yet the more consistent and perhaps tougher-minded "rationalists" of the sixties and seventies had no such misgivings. Like Professor Ptthmllsprts in *The Water-babies*, they had little doubt that they could adequately describe man in "scientific" terms as a simple fact of nature and so dispel his every degrading illusion of divinity.

If the sanguine Professor lacked the intellectual subtlety of John Stuart Mill, he was nonetheless a Utilitarian in practice and perhaps even a Millite in theory. For Mill by the sixties had established himself as the major Victorian "rationalist," as the one most determined to qualify each proposition with the

[5] See Leonard Huxley, ed., *Life and Letters of Thomas Henry Huxley* (New York, 1916), II, 249, 401.
[6] See Pearson, *The Ethic of Freethought* (1883: London, 1901), p. 9.
[7] Quoted by John Morley, *On Compromise* (1874: London, 1928), p. 161n.
[8] See Hutton, *op. cit.*, I, 298.

fullest possible evidence of provable fact, to approach psychology and ethics with the empirical bias of the laboratory scientist and with a like will to measure results in a mood of cool disinterest. Despite his late essays on religion, which his followers deeply regretted, he seemed in many respects the perfect prototype of the agnostic of the seventies—the agnostic described by Leslie Stephen as one who, unlike the pantheist or the pessimist, found himself unable to regard the universe "with any but a colourless emotion."[9] Whatever the manifest contradictions of his philosophy, he was, at least for the last decade of his life, the most influential of British thinkers. Yet his thought proved of little solace to Tennyson, and his influence upon literature, generally, remained almost negligible. For few men of letters, seeking a scale of value, an aesthetic criterion, could find a real utility in his guarded detachment, his willing suspension of belief.

Not many of Mill's fellow-"rationalists," however, could match his dispassionate logic. Morley and Stephen, Tyndall, Harrison and Huxley all mitigated their "rationalism" by a faith—highly irrational on their own agnostic premises—in the sanctity of human nature, a faith borrowed directly, though involuntarily, from the Evangelical theology they had rejected. Adapting to his own uses a vocabulary of religious connotation, Tyndall applauded "the inexorable advance of man's understanding in the path of knowledge" and "the immortal victories which science has won for the human race."[10] And Morley, aflame as he was with ethical emotion—a queer amalgam, said Harrison, of Diderot and John Wesley[11]—preached the holiness of man's reason, "the surest and most potent of our weapons" in a "life-long battle against the forces of darkness."[12] Both Morley and Huxley resisted Comte's deification of the human race as a

---

[9] See Stephen, *An Agnostic's Apology and other Essays* (London, 1893), p. 18.
[10] Tyndall, *The Advancement of Science* (New York, 1874), pp. 86-87.
[11] Harrison, quoted by Warren Staebler, *The Liberal Mind of John Morley* (Princeton, 1943), p. 44.
[12] Morley, *On Compromise*, p. 116.

sacred entity, a Great Being or rather Goddess; but the Religion of Humanity was nonetheless the logical result of an illogical reverence for the "scientific" method. And to Harrison, at any rate, the new creed with its dogmas and rituals, its secular saints and "rational" sacraments, its "Catholicism minus Christianity," seemed the ultimate expression of the great Positive Synthesis, satisfying alike to mind and soul. Within a few years the faithful under his guidance would gather for "congregational worship" at Newton Hall in Fetter Lane. There they might admire "a large copy of the Sistine Madonna and busts of the great men of all ages from Moses to Bichat, whose names are in the New Calendar," or chant humanistic hymns to the accompaniment of a grand piano, once the property of Charles Darwin.[13] But though Harrison could commend verses by George Eliot as suitable for Positivist service, the new religion in its orthodox form scarcely touched the literary imagination. It assuredly furnished no philosophic basis for a renaissance of poetry. For it presented certain obvious difficulties to the critical and creative intelligence. R. H. Hutton, acute in both theology and letters, rightly questioned the Positivist aspiration "to reconcile in man the sceptical mind and the believing heart," to combine "all the meditative ecstasy of those who wished to live in God, with the cold conviction of the student of mere phenomena that there was no God to live in." And many another late Victorian, convinced that the "reconciliation" had been achieved only by the outright surrender of intellect to emotion, might join in Hutton's complaint that "the attempt to love a *Grand Être,* or even a *Déesse,* in the existence of which the mind does not believe, must always be a futile one, which only men of more fancy than realism, or some lesion of the brain, will be able to accomplish."[14] If the Religion of Humanity, then, was the end-product of a "scientific rationalism," it seemed clear that the "rationalists" had succeeded only in destroying reason.

[13] On Newton Hall and the Positivist religion, see Frederic Harrison, *Autobiographic Memoirs* (London, 1911), II, 260-291.
[14] Hutton, *op. cit.,* I, 307, 308-309.

Long before the extremes of the Positive Synthesis were manifest in England, however, the "rationalistic" position was already being subjected to organized attack. On coming up to Oxford in 1870 H. H. Asquith had found a growing "idealistic revolt, or reaction" slowly undermining the once almost undisputed influence of Mill.[15] And by the end of the seventies Leslie Stephen felt called upon to defend his agnostic stand against "this idealism of a newer fashion."[16] Impressed by the speculations of Hegel, the new idealists, especially T. H. Green, F. H. Bradley, and the brothers Caird, were proceeding to assail the first premises of Utilitarian doctrine. All attacked not science itself, but "the philosophy which claimed that science was the only kind of knowledge that ever existed or ever could exist."[17] And all sought to reassert the permanency of human values on a higher plane than scientific induction could reach.

While the "rationalists," bent upon the analysis of matter, had tended to discount mind, the British idealists concentrated attention upon the mental processes which constituted the dynamic world of forms behind all the appearances of fact. In his *Ethical Studies* of 1876, Bradley, who was perhaps their major spokesman, repudiated the "rationalistic" creeds of his contemporaries with a logic somewhat more assertive than Hutton's, but no less urbane and ironic. Mill, he argued, began by accepting pleasure as the single good, soon found his instincts telling him that he must live for others, and so concluded that the pleasure of others must be the object of living. But this, said Bradley, "is not a good theoretical deduction; . . . it is the generation of the Utilitarian monster, and of that we must say that its heart is in the right place but the brain is wanting."[18] Yet the progeny of Positivism seemed scarcely more reasonable; for "humanity" in the abstract was but "the name of an imaginary

---

[15] See Asquith, *Some Aspects of the Victorian Age* (Oxford, 1918), p. 17.
[16] Stephen, quoted by Helen H. Young, *The Writings of Walter Pater* (Lancaster, Pa., 1933), p. 14.
[17] R. G. Collingwood, *The Idea of History* (Oxford, 1946), p. 134.
[18] Bradley, *Ethical Studies* (London, 1876), p. 104.

collection," and even if "humanity" were an entity possessed of "a real self-sameness," it could not—being one finite phenomenon—serve as the object of a satisfactory religion.[19] Nor did Matthew Arnold's "rational" theology with its talk of a "power not ourselves that makes for righteousness" appear to Bradley other than vague and evasive. "We must not," he wrote, "be ashamed to say that we fail to understand what any one of these phrases mean and suspect ourselves once more to be on the scent of clap-trap."[20]

Here, then, in the *Ethical Studies,* Hutton or even Newman might have found a hostility to secular creeds not far removed from his own. Here Tennyson, had he known it, might have seen a formal rebuke to the "experts" who dismissed his intuitions. But when Bradley turned from an attack on "rationalism" to a closer articulation of his basic premises, he was forced to enter realms of epistemology into which only the trained philosopher, familiar with the specialized language of his profession, could venture to follow him. His later work, particularly the *Appearance and Reality* of 1893, developed the concept of "mind as process" in terms which effectively destroyed the lingering notion of "mind as substance" and so prepared the way for the realists and pragmatists of the twentieth century.[21] Yet by the end of the Victorian era the new philosophy, like the new theoretical physics, was no longer the property of the common man. Not entirely without dispassion could Harrison complain that truth was being obscured rather than revealed by the "Neo-Hegelian fumes" of British idealism.[22] For in order to resolve in a new synthesis the manifold contradictions of modern thought, Green and Bradley and their followers had of necessity to sacrifice the gift of popular speech, a gift which the "rationalists," Harrison and Morley, Huxley and Stephen, had held in full measure. Though they struggled to assert an ethic for

[19] Bradley, *op. cit.,* pp. 305-307n.
[20] *Ibid.,* p. 283.
[21] See Charles W. Morris, *Six Theories of Mind* (Chicago, 1932), pp. 47, 76, 77.
[22] Harrison, *op. cit.,* I, 136.

democracy, their influence was confined largely to the academic circles whence it had arisen. The average late-Victorian writer scarcely suspected that in their work lay a reaffirmation of many of the values from which an earlier Victorian culture had derived its strength.

Unmoved by the appeals of Green and Bradley, a good many young men of the seventies nonetheless sensed the inadequacy of a "scientific rationalism," and a number, disillusioned and bewildered, openly ridiculed all the moralities formulated in the name of reason. In literature the nimblest of the younger wits was undoubtedly W. H. Mallock, who was already anticipating in various ways the disenchantment of the nineties. Mallock at the outset saw in parody and burlesque-romance the perfect media for exposing the fallacies of intellectual "liberalism" without for the moment committing himself to any less absurd belief. Published in 1877, his *New Republic* was a symposium in the manner of Peacock, loosely fashioned to bring together under transparent disguises the intellectual leaders of the day, such diverse figures as Arnold, Jowett, Tyndall, Pater, Huxley, Clifford, each of whom in the course of the garrulous house-party might voice his own earnest credo and in so doing inadvertently betray the folly of his conviction. Though less brilliantly executed, Mallock's *New Paul and Virginia, or Positivism on an Island,* which followed a year later, was both more coherent in structure and more specific in attack. Practised in the idiom of Tyndall and of Harrison, the shipwrecked hero, Professor Paul Darnley, almost succeeds in converting to Positivism his desert-island mate, Virginia Saint John, an Anglo-Catholic lady affianced to the Bishop of the Chasuble Islands. But when at the crucial moment a rescue-party interrupts his instructions, Virginia returns joyfully to her bishop, and Paul at the sight of his wife recovers his belief in hell. For in the last analysis, we are left to deduce, Positivism can withstand neither the onslaught of passion nor the test of grim experience.

From Mallock's serious writings we may gauge the mental

attitude that underlay his hostility to all the liberal Victorian thinkers. At Oxford he had been, as he tells us, antagonized by every shade of "free thought"; yet he never advanced to the transcendental metaphysic of Green, which might well have provided the interplay of intellect and emotion that his spirit seemed to require. Instead, he turned virtually against the intelligence itself; and what he at first conceived to be a revolt from middle-class standards soon became a completely blind reaction to the whole progress of modern knowledge. Socially, aesthetically, politically, he sought refuge from "the wintry actualities of today" in a feudal past remote from the din of democracy. His novels dedicated to the propagation of a "scientific conservatism" were in effect their own parodies. Even in furniture his taste was, he confessed, less artistic than political, for the kind of chair that best pleased him was "one that had been made and used before the first Reform Bill."[23] He lived all for lordly hospitality and antique manners; and at the end of his life when he could no longer actively propagandize the virtue of reaction, he could still find an antidote to despair in the gossip of polite society or, despite the threat of personal want, lose himself once more in the long and complex annals of the rich.

Mallock's contempt for the aspirations of the Philistines and his respect for the leisured graces of the *beau monde* were shared by the "dandies" of the Decadence, the heroes of the Wildean drama. Yet his general distrust of the free intelligence was common to a rather large group of late Victorians who felt no comparable interest in the social amenities. If the revolt from "rationalism" awakened in him a nostalgia for the outward forms of a lost culture, it led others to "reaction" on less material planes. It helped perhaps prepare an audience for the anti-intellectual philosophy of Schopenhauer, at last becoming available in English translation. It was probably a factor in shaping

---

[23] Mallock, *Memoirs of Life and Literature* (New York, 1920), p. 160.

the bitterness of Thomas Hardy and a force behind the cosmic pessimism of James Thomson. It increased the vogue of popular novelists like "Ouida" who provided a welcome retreat from the restive intellect by exploiting mere sensation untrammeled by moral purpose. It carried the ebullient Laurence Oliphant from the composition of his bright satiric *Piccadilly* to the practice of a perverse sexual mysticism in Palestinian Haifa.[24] And it encouraged a widespread interest in spiritualistic revelation which made possible the frauds of Madame Blavatsky and the founding of the somewhat more respectable Society for Psychical Research.

Confronted by the barren certainties of "scientific rationalism," the literary artist of the seventies who was unable to return to an orthodox faith or to discover a satisfactory substitute philosophy was driven more and more into a world of private symbols. He was forced increasingly, as Pater explained, to turn in upon himself, where "in the narrow cell of its own subjective experience, the action of a powerful nature [would] be intense, but exclusive and peculiar." Under such circumstances, the man of sensibility, no longer troubled like Tennsyon by the inductions of the "experts," would become the self-sufficient Aesthete, the devotee of a determined art for art's sake. Then "the vocation of the artist, of the student of life or books," said Pater, would "be realised with something—say! of fanaticism, as an end in itself, unrelated, unassociated." And his art accordingly would be deprived forever of what Pater in his least "aesthetic" mood called "that sense of large proportion in things, that all-embracing prospect of life as a whole."[25]

By the seventies, for better or for worse, a personal impressionism, self-consciously "aesthetic" in its avowals, had begun in all the arts to eclipse the social concern of the high Vic-

[24] On Oliphant, see Herbert W. Schneider and George Lawton, *A Prophet and a Pilgrim*, . . . *Thomas Lake Harris and Laurence Oliphant* (New York, 1942).
[25] Pater, "Prosper Mérimée" (1890), *Miscellaneous Studies* (New York, 1895), pp. 2-3.

torians. Morley who had at first hailed the new "aesthetic interest"[26] as a healthy protest against the faith of the Philistines, soon saw that no specialized interest operating in isolation could further the ends of the "liberal" culture he desired. The Victorian Age, he complained at last, had profited little by "forsaking the clerical idyll of one school, for the reactionary medievalism or paganism, intrinsically meaningless and issueless, of another."[27] For the Aesthetes, alienated from the old ideals of life and art and heedless of the new idealism, remained of necessity "reactionaries," quite unresponsive to the argument of "rationalism" which had offered them no tenable aesthetic criterion. And it was ultimately clear to Morley and his friends that each subjective credo that animated with its own gemlike flame the art-for-art's-sake movement had arisen directly from the artist's calculated indifference to the force of general ideas.

[26] See Edwin M. Everett, *The Party of Humanity* (Chapel Hill, N. C., 1939), p. 243.
[27] See Morley, "Byron" (1887), *Critical Miscellanies* (London, 1923), p. 129.

JEROME HAMILTON BUCKLEY

The University of Wisconsin

VII

The Tragedy in Little Hintock
New Light on Thomas Hardy's Novel *The Woodlanders*

Q UEEN VICTORIA acceded to the throne in June, 1837. Fifty years later the Golden Jubilee of this occasion was celebrated throughout England. On "Jubilee night" a man who was later to become known as the author of one of the most popular books of English poetry produced during the Victorian period, the then-unknown A. E. Housman, walked from his home at Bromsgrove, Fockbury House, to the top of a nearby hill, and there watched the bonfires burning—the "beacons" he afterwards wrote about in Poem Number One in *A Shropshire Lad:*

> Look left, look right, the hills are bright,
> The dales are light between,
> Because 'tis fifty years to-night
> That God has saved the Queen.

At that same time, another beacon in Queen Victoria's galaxy of literary stars, Thomas Hardy, was seated with his wife in the Savile Club in London, watching the royal procession go down Piccadilly. He had recently returned from a spring tour of Italy, and was now pausing in London long enough, not only to take in the Queen's Jubilee, but also to make certain revisions in the text of a recent book. Sixty years have since passed, but in all that time those revisions have never, so far as I know, been examined by any student of Victorian literature. The present paper will attempt to correct that omission.

A few weeks after the celebration of Queen Victoria's Jubilee, Robert Louis Stevenson came up from Bournemouth and was in London on Sunday the twenty-first of August, 1887, preparing to sail the next day on his last departure from England. Friends were on hand to see him off. Edmund Gosse was long able to remember the day, because the only books that Stevenson wished to carry away with him were the three volumes of Thomas Hardy's newly published novel *The Woodlanders,* and (since none of the friends had a copy) Gosse was called upon to find one. The bookshops were, of course, closed on Sunday and Gosse's resourcefulness was challenged. Eventually, however, he found a set of the green-backed books, "borrowed or stolen somewhere," and Stevenson was able to sail on the morrow, equipped with reading-matter for the voyage. While crossing the Atlantic, he read to Mrs. Stevenson (or she to him) the forty-eight chapters of the novel, and by the time that the *Ludgate Hill* docked at New York, Stevenson was ready to agree with John A. Steuart's verdict that "such a book as *The Woodlanders* is enough to make one feel proud of one's generation."

If Stevenson had been a subscriber to *Macmillan's Magazine,* he might have read *The Woodlanders* without putting Gosse to so much trouble on that memorable Sunday. The novel began its serial appearance in the magazine in May, 1886, and ran through April, 1887. Hardy composed the novel by installments during its publication, and did not complete his task until as late as February of 1887. As soon as the April issue of the magazine[1] was in print, Macmillan & Company rushed the text of the entire novel into type for a conventional three-volume First

---

[1] *Macmillan's* was no fledgling. It had opened its career in November, 1859, only a few weeks before the publication of Darwin's *Origin of Species,* and it continued its monthly appearances for forty-eight years.

Edition, which made its appearance on March 15. Stevenson had therefore had five months in which to acquire *The Woodlanders* in book form, but his awareness that he was about to leave England, perhaps for the last time, doubtless gave him many other problems more important, or more insistent, than acquiring a copy of *The Woodlanders*. Before the end of the month in which he sailed for America, Macmillian & Company issued a second edition in one volume—in fact, two editions: one for sale in England, the other (No. 49 in "Macmillan's Colonial Library") for sale in Canada, Australia, and other British dominions.

By the time that Stevenson reached New York, *The Woodlanders* had already become widely known to readers in the United States. Hardy's American publishers, Harper & Brothers, had received "advance sheets" of *Macmillan's Magazine* and were thus enabled to issue the novel on March 25, only ten days after its appearance in London. Harpers, like Macmillan in London, issued *The Woodlanders* in two different forms: it was published as No. 572 in Harper's "Franklin Square Library," at a price of twenty cents, and was published in book form at seventy-five cents. There had been no serial publication in America, though Hardy had written to Thomas Bailey Aldrich as early as November 27, 1885, to try to sell *The Woodlanders* to the *Atlantic Monthly*, of which Aldrich was then editor.[2] The Boston periodical did not buy; but there was, at this time, another way by which a novel was often brought to the attention of thousands of American readers other than by magazine publication. That way was through one or another of the cheap "Libraries" published by a number of American

[2] The correspondence between Hardy and Aldrich has been printed in my book, *Hardy in America* (Waterville, Maine: Colby College Press), 1946. See page 85. Other references throughout this article are reduced to a minimum, in order not to clutter it up with footnotes. The curious reader wishing specific documentation for my allusions to, or quotations from, Abercrombie, Blunden, Chew, Rutland, etc., will find it given in my compilation *The First Hundred Years of Thomas Hardy: A Centenary Bibliography of Hardiana* (Waterville, Maine: Colby College Library, 1942).

houses. The "Lakeside Library" of Donnelley, Loyd & Company in Chicago, the "Fireside Library" of Beadle & Adams, and the "Seaside Library" of George Munro in New York are merely three of a large number of extended series of unauthorized American publications, issued by publishers who, by helping themselves to whatever British wares they wished and by printing on the cheapest kind of paper, were able to offer books by English novelists for twenty, or ten, or even five cents.[8] Hardy received the uninvited services of these enterprising gentlemen. Within three weeks of the time when Harpers made *The Woodlanders* available in their Franklin Square Library, the products of the piratical printing presses began to appear on the market in New York. George Munro's "Seaside" edition was dated April 16, 1887; Norman Munro's twenty-cent edition followed only two weeks later; and John W. Lovell had another twenty-cent edition ready by May 7. At the time of Robert Louis Stevenson's arrival in New York, *The Woodlanders* was already available in five different American garbs; and later on, A. L. Burt, Rand McNally, Peter F. Collier, the Hovendon Company, the International Book Company, George Munro's Sons, Street & Smith, the United States Book Company, R. F. Fenno, and the Fifth Avenue Publishing Company added at least a dozen more American editions to the supply. In New York Hardy's novel enjoyed no copyright protection: none was possible under the law in 1887.

This commercial and legal fact has had surprising but little-understood results, not only in Hardy's day, at the time of the first publication of the novel, but throughout the subsequent sixty years, down to the moment of the present investigation. When Macmillan & Company published *The Woodlanders* in London, it was greeted with enthusiastic and almost unanimous acclaim; but the American response to the cheaply-printed story showed no such unanimity of opinion. In London the *Athe-*

[8] For details see Chapter III, "The Pirates on the Hudson," in *Hardy in America*.

naeum declared that *The Woodlanders* "should be read by all who can tell masterly work in fiction when they see it." The *Saturday Review* announced that this novel (particularly the second of the three volumes) contained some of the best writing that Hardy had ever done. In *The Academy* (in what Edmund Blunden has recently called "the ablest of the reviews" of *The Woodlanders*—"that written . . . by William Wallace, the philosopher"), the statement was made that *"The Woodlanders* is decidedly the best and most powerful work Mr. Hardy has produced since *Far from the Madding Crowd."* This means that Wallace put it ahead, not only of *The Trumpet-Major* and *Two on a Tower,* but also of *The Return of the Native* and *The Mayor of Casterbridge.*

The professional reviewers and critics were not the only ones in England to hail *The Woodlanders.* When Alfred Austin, shortly before he became Poet Laureate, published his *Love's Widowhood* (1889), he sent Hardy a copy with an inscription "To the Author of *The Woodlanders."* Later British writers and critics continued to express hearty approval of this work. Annie Macdonell, writing in 1894, thought that "the book deserves a high place," and Lascelles Abercrombie expressed the judgment (in 1912) that *"The Woodlanders* is full of a profound penetration" and that Marty South, one of the characters that give the book its special quality, "is by far the greatest and noblest of Hardy's types of simple-natured womanhood." Sir Arthur Quiller-Couch, a discriminating reader of Hardy's novels, called *The Woodlanders* "to my thinking his loveliest if not his strongest book." Arnold Bennett went even further. "If I had to name the finest English novel," he once declared, "I should undoubtedly choose *The Woodlanders."* Modern English critics have continued to agree with these judgments. "Of the Wessex novels," writes Cyril Aldred, *"The Woodlanders* is, perhaps, the most balanced and satisfying work." William R. Rutland declares: "There are many to-day who would say that it [*The Woodlanders*] is Hardy's best novel. . . . The many merits and beauties of the book have been so often praised that there is no need to do it again at length."

When, now, we turn from this prolonged chorus of praise in England to our own side of the ocean, we find the reception accorded *The Woodlanders* marked by sharp disagreement. The *Atlantic Monthly* ignored the novel altogether. Aldrich, having refused to buy it for serialization in the Boston magazine, perhaps thought it wise to refrain altogether from critical comment on the rejected work. Harper & Brothers, who published *The Woodlanders,* of course had a magazine of their own in which they could puff their wares, and in *Harper's* the new novel was twice called to the attention of readers. In June, 1887, Laurence Hutton wrote of it pleasantly and singled Marty South out for praise as "a Woodlander pure and simple," whose admirable character "reaches almost to a point of sublimity." A month later Editor Henry M. Alden reported having read "Mr. Hardy's *Woodlanders* . . . with the enjoyment that all his books give us," and assured readers that, if they tried this latest novel—the *first* to be published (in book form) by Harper & Brothers—they would "be rewarded with pleasures which no one but Thomas Hardy is able to impart." But other American critics sounded a different note. The editor of the *Literary World,* while admitting that "the incomparable touch of a master's hand is perceptible on every page and in every line of *The Woodlanders*," still thought the dominant note to be bitter, unpleasantly so. "*The Woodlanders* is a disagreeable novel; there is no disguising this melancholy conclusion. It leaves the reader . . . baffled, stupefied, cast down." The reviewer in *The Nation,* who had received a copy, not of the book in "half-cloth" priced at seventy-five cents, but of the twenty-cent "Franklin Square Library" edition on poor paper, with small type, and narrow, crowded columns, felt none of that sublimity which Laurence Hutton had found in Marty South, and thought that Hardy was merely "over tender with a girl who affects us unpleasantly, like a noxious weed. . . . Grace Melbury . . . takes all she can get . . . , by fair means or foul. . . . The principal events . . . lead us to infer that Woodlanders are as bad as other people and even worse; and . . . Marty South and Winterborne are dull examples of virtue. . . ."

It is impossible not to suspect that a cheap opinion of the novel was encouraged in the minds of some American critics by the cheap appearance of the book. Its unattractive format made it difficult to believe that "the finest English novel" had been ushered thus into the world. But the American critical response to *The Woodlanders* involved more than mere format, for in many ways the *text* of the American edition was inferior to the text of the London edition. It has never been pointed out, up to the moment of my writing these words, that the novel as printed in New York in 1887, and as reprinted there for thirty or forty years thereafter, was not the same novel as printed in London. Not that both were not called *The Woodlanders,* not that both did not tell the tragic story of Giles Winterborne and record the loyal love of Marty South, but in many ways the New York and the London texts differed—and differed at points and in ways that could easily influence critical judgment. If the conversation between Giles and Grace Melbury is stilted and artificial and unconvincing in a New York text, whereas in a London copy of the book it is simple and natural and easy, the American reader will find it hard to respond to Grace sympathetically, whereas the British reader will be led into a tolerant understanding of Grace's difficult position. And, by reason of the publishing conditions which existed in 1887, this is exactly what happened. Let me recall some of the facts.

From 1873 through 1886, Henry Holt had been Thomas Hardy's authorized publisher in America; but in the latter year, "by an amicable arrangement," Holt had ceded all claims to and rights in Hardy's work to Harper & Brothers, and Hardy had accordingly been notified that they would be the ones to bring out the new novel in America, as soon as it had ended its run in *Macmillan's Magazine.* The twelfth and last installment appeared in the issue for April, 1887. Copies of the pages in which the novel was printed were sent to Harpers in advance, and from these "advance sheets" they set up their own type, preparatory to issuing their own edition of the novel. Aware of the likelihood that the pirates would swoop down, the minute the new ship unfurled its sails, Harpers dared not wait for last-minute corrections and revisions. They stuck to the text of the London serialization and had their own book ready in New York ten days after the publication of the Macmillan book in London.

Their fears were realized. There were eventually at least nineteen unauthorized printings of the novel.[4] The text of all nineteen was, of course, taken from the Harper edition of 1887. After that initial publication, Harper & Brothers re-issued *The Woodlanders* from time to time—in 1896, for example, and in 1900; in 1905 and 1910; in 1917 and 1926—all these editions being really mere reprints, not new "editions" in a strict sense, for they were all, without exception, printed from the plates of the original 1887 edition. They thus preserved intact the text of the novel as it had appeared in *Macmillan's Magazine*. By 1926 there had thus appeared in America at least ten Harper printings of *The Woodlanders*, plus one edition (P. F. Collier's) published by special arrangement with Harpers, plus at least nineteen unauthorized editions. All thirty retained without change the wording of the original London serialization.

This statement takes on a more surprising aspect when it is put negatively: not one of these thirty American editions printed the text as Hardy wished it to be printed. For not one paid any attention to any of the revisions he made, and had made even before the First Edition was published in London. No American edition has ever reproduced the text of the first English edition. No American edition has ever reproduced the text of the second English edition, which appeared in August, 1887, shortly after Stevenson's departure from England. Hardy made revisions in the text of the novel before Macmillan set up the type for the

[4] The individual imprints are given in a check-list appended to this article.

first edition, and he made additional revisions almost immediately after the British public had made clear, by the acclaim with which they greeted the first edition, that a second would soon be wanted. Eight years later, when a Uniform Collected Edition of all the Wessex Novels (for publication by Osgood, McIlvaine & Company) was prepared in London, Hardy wrote a preface for *The Woodlanders* and again revised the text. But—surprising though this discovery may be—even then Harpers continued to print from their original plates. They issued a set of Hardy's works corresponding to the Osgood set issued in London, but they did not take over the Osgood text. As far as *The Woodlanders* is concerned, no American edition has ever reproduced the text of the Osgood edition. Is not this surprising? Thirty American printings of *The Woodlanders,* but not one that gives a reader access to Hardy's revisions of March, 1887, or of June, 1887, or of September, 1895!

In April, 1912, Hardy went over the text of the novel for the last time—deciding at that time that, "as a story," he liked *The Woodlanders* best of all his novels. He made these his final revisions for publication in the "Wessex Edition" issued in London by Macmillan & Company in 1912.[5] Had he been aware (as he was *not*) that throughout the preceding quarter of a century, none of his numerous American readers had been able to benefit by the care that he had shown in trying to polish off his text to the artistic perfection his critical sense admired, had he been aware of this sad fact, he would doubtless have taken belated joy in learning from his London publishers that—at last, in 1912—his New York publishers were going to import plates of the definitive London edition and that American readers would thus—at last!—be able to read the novel in the most approved form. But alas, when Harpers acquired from London their set of the 1912 plates, they published exactly 153 copies of their "Auto-

---

[5] This London "Wessex Edition" should be carefully distinguished from the American "Wessex Edition" published by Harpers in 1900 and repeated by them (in a different binding) in 1905.

graph Edition." One hundred and fifty-three Americans, by buying the entire set of Hardy's works, were able, in 1912, to acquire the definitive text of *The Woodlanders*. Not many colleges or universities were numbered among the hundred and fifty-three. Nine years later, the situation was somewhat improved by the publication of the "Anniversary Edition" of Hardy's works (New York, 1921: it was the fiftieth anniversary of the publication of Hardy's first novel); but again, only those who bought an entire set could acquire *The Woodlanders* with all the revisions of 1887-1912. Not until Thomas Hardy had died, in January, 1928, did his American publishers finally make easily available, in their current "trade edition," a copy of *The Woodlanders* with the author's definitive text.

It is clear from the foregoing account that Hardy followed a prolonged and consistent process of revision—a process that began with the composition of the manuscript in 1885-1887, and arrived at the definitive text by four subsequent steps. What this means is that *The Woodlanders* exists in five different textual states, and that of thirty-five different American editions (or printings), thirty give only the first of these five states, none give the second, third, or fourth states; and of five recent American editions that do print the definitive text, two are so rare as to be generally inaccessible, two others are out of print, and only one—one edition out of the fifty cited in the appended check-list—is easily available. To put these findings in tidy form, here is the record:

I. The original manuscript (which is now in the Dorset County Museum in Dorchester) provided the text as serialized in *Macmillan's Magazine*, which produced

  (a) Eleven legitimate offspring, all American (numbered 2, 3, 17, 23, 25, 31, 32, 33, 35, 40, and 45 in the appended check-list); and
  (b) nineteen illegitimate offspring, all American (numbered 4, 5, 6, 9, 11, 12, 13, 14, 15, 18, 19, 20, 21, 22, 24, 26, 27, 28, and 30).

II. Revisions of the magazine text, made by March, 1887, were published in the first edition, London (No. 1 in the check-list). No American edition contains this version.

III. Revisions made in (or about) June, 1887, produced Numbers 7, 8, and 10. None of these are American.

IV. A preface written in September, 1895, and further revisions made for the Osgood edition of 1896 produced Numbers 16, 29, 34, 38, 39, 44, 48, and 49. None of these are American.

V. Final revisions, together with an addition to the preface, were made in April, 1912; these appear in Numbers 36, 37 (only 153 copies), 41, 42, 43, 46, 47, and 50. Number 46 (or more recent reprints of it in 1930 and 1938) is therefore the sole American edition with the definitive text available to any large number of American readers. Unfortunately this one is *not* the one found in the libraries of most American colleges and universities.

Students of Hardy's novels who receive this information will naturally wonder just what difference there is in the texts of these five differing versions. In a brief report such as is here offered, one cannot provide a detailed study of the forty-eight chapters of the novel, but a few instructive examples can be given.

Hardy's revision was sometimes a very slight matter—a change in a phrase or a clause, such as that made, for example, in the reference to "a residence on the hill-side" at the beginning of Chapter III: "of which there is nothing to say at present." This is the dull negative statement that Hardy wrote in his manuscript, and this unexciting negation is found in all the defective American editions. But the first edition in London changed the negative to a positive statement. It reads: "of which there is something to be said later on." The second edition further identified the residence as "that of the young medical gentleman . . . , of whom there is something to be said later on." But for forty years American editions ignored these improvements.

In English editions the Doctor's name was Edred Fitzpiers; in American editions, it was Edgar. Winterborne met him "near Reveller's Inn" in the London text, but "at Calfhay Cross" in New York editions. London readers were told that Mrs. Charmond traveled "to Homburg," whereas Americans read that she went "to Baden." At Heidelberg she lost her gloves, according to the New York text; but in London the statement was that she lost her handkerchief. American readers were told that "some person who had just come from Sherton entered . . . with the news that Mr. Fitzpiers . . . had been seen hiring a carriage at the Earl of Wessex Hotel," but the British edition mentioned, instead, the King's Arms Hotel at Casterbridge. In New York, readers learned of "the old stone-fronted inn with a yawning arch," but in England the text referred to "the 'Earl of Wessex' —a substantial inn of Ham-hill stone with a yawning back yard." According to the New York version, the stone came "from local quarries," but the London text says "From Ham-hill quarries." One London critic questioned the necessity of telling the reader that the Earl of Wessex Hotel had "been rebuilt," but the American reader was not given that information; the New York text stated that the hotel had been "enlarged."

These details are, of course, not vital; none of them changed the course of the tragedy or transformed the character of any of the actors. But others of Hardy's revisions *are* vital: for example, the two sentences at the end of Chapter XX—two sentences which are *not* present in the American text from 1887 to 1926:

(1) Fitzpiers kissed her [Suke Damson] again, and pressed her close to him.
(2) It was daybreak before Fitzpiers and Suke Damson re-entered Little Hintock.

Consider the difference in the effectiveness of the two texts: the London reader fully informed of the episode with Suke; the American reader denied these two telling sentences.

It has long been a commonplace of Hardy criticism to speak of the poetic quality of his style, particularly in descriptive passages, and of his unrivaled skill in setting the present against a nostalgic vista of the past. In view of this fact, it will be of particular interest to observe how passages which illustrate these notable qualities of Hardy's style differ in the two texts. I select two sentences from the first chapter in order to illustrate the striking contrast between what the American reader was offered and what the reader in London was offered.

In the original Harper version, the text read: "At one place, where a hill is crossed, the largest of the woods shows itself bisected by the highway, as the head of thick hair is bisected by the white line of its parting." No English edition of *The Woodlanders* has ever been published with this trivial simile of the head of thick hair. But thirty American editions have it! In England the sentence beginning "At one place" appears in four different versions—records of Hardy's repeated efforts at improvement of his text. In the first edition the sentence read: "At one place, where Rubdon Hill is crossed, a bank slopes up to the trees on the left hand, while on the right spreads a deep and silent vale." The bank and the deep and silent vale did not last very long. In the second edition, five months later, the sentence was changed to read: "At one place, the north side of Rubdon Hill, the leaves lie so thick in autumn as to completely bury the track." Eight years later Hardy replaced Rubdon Hill with High-Stoy Hill, and in the Osgood edition of 1896 the sentence reads: "At one place, on the outskirts of Blackmoor Vale, where the bold brow of High-Stoy Hill is seen a mile or two ahead, the leaves lie so thick in autumn as to completely bury the track."[6] This version was allowed to remain, except that, in 1912, Hardy changed "a mile or two ahead" to read "two or three miles ahead." The final wording of the sentence is indeed a far cry from the head of thick hair bisected by the white line of its parting.

The second sentence selected from Chapter I, a sentence that again illustrates Hardy's tentative method of composition, has to do with the same hill—"a hill," in New York; "Rubdon Hill,"

---

[6] The split infinitive remained unchanged; it is still there in the definitive text. As Lionel Johnson remarked in 1894, Hardy was "an inveterate patron of the split infinitive."

in London, at first, and later "High-Stoy Hill." The manuscript version, reproduced in the Harper texts from 1887 to 1926, reads: "The dead men's work that had been expended in climbing that hill, the blistered soles that had trodden it, and the tears that had wetted it, were not his concern." Again a negative statement. Hardy was satisfied with the "blistered soles" and the "tears that had wetted" the highway, but nothing else about the sentence continued long to suit him. He removed "the dead men," shifted the sentence to another paragraph, and in the first edition made the sentence read: "The many gay ones now perished who have rolled over the hill, the blistered soles that have trodden it, and the tears that have wetted it, return upon the mind...." In the second edition, "gay ones" was changed to "gay charioteers." In 1896 "over the hill" was changed to "along the way." In the edition of 1912 no further revision of this sentence was made; it therefore read: "The many gay charioteers now perished who have rolled along the way . . . return upon the mind." But in New York, down to 1926, "the dead men's work" continued to be "not his concern."

Even more striking—and more vitally important—than revisions like these just quoted are those that make a decided change in the characterization or in the development of the plot. Take, for example, the characterizing power of the dialogue in Chapter VI. In the American version, Grace Melbury and Giles Winterborne carry on the following wooden and stilted conversation:

"Do you ever look at things philosophically instead of personally?" she [Grace] asked.

"I can't say that I do," answered Giles, his eyes lingering far ahead upon a dark spot, which proved to be a brougham.

"I think you may, sometimes, with advantage," said she. "Look at yourself as a pitcher drifting on the stream [of time] with other pitchers, and consider what contrivances are most desirable for avoiding cracks in general, and not only for saving your poor one. Shall I tell you all about Bath.... ?"

Hardy came to realize that talk like this was entirely out of character—that no "woodlanders" would ever converse this way—and accordingly he changed the passage to read thus in the definitive edition:

"But old feelings come to life again in some people," she added softly.
"And in others they have never died!" said he.
"Ah—they are Love's very *ownest* and best, I suppose! I don't pretend to rank so high as they.
"It's not a they—it's a he."
Grace sighed. "Shall I tell you all about Brighton. . . . ?"

Many of the changes which we have been noting were made by Hardy as far back as the spring of 1887—revisions which appear in the three-volume first edition. But some of the most important changes were made later. A good example of Hardy's persistent efforts to improve his text may be found in the last chapter. Five pages from the end of the novel there is a passage that describes Melbury's reactions to the discovery, made by Melbury's companions, that Grace had rejoined her husband. The passage originally ran: "Melbury himself, restless as usual, walked to the door while he waited for them, and looked up and down the street. 'I'd gie her a good shaking, if she were my maid, . . .' said a bark-ripper. . . ." This version appears in the first edition (London, 1887), but in June of that same year Hardy added two sentences which appeared in the second edition (August, 1887). Between the two sentences quoted above, he inserted: " 'Well—he's her husband,' Melbury said to himself. 'But it's a forlorn hope for her; and God knows how it will end!' " But even this did not satisfy him. Readers let Hardy know that the point was not made clear to them.[7] To make certain that no one would fail to grasp Melbury's meaning and its

---

[7] This passage in *The Woodlanders* was the subject of a conversation between Hardy and Miss Rebekah Owen of New York City. I have reported it in an article, "Hardy and *The Woodlanders*," in the *Review of English Studies*, XV (1939), 330-333.

full significance, Hardy made a further insertion. In the Osgood edition of 1896, just before "But it's a forlorn hope," he added: "and let her take him back to her bed if she will! But let her bear in mind that the woman walks and laughs somewhere at this very moment whose neck he'll be coling next year as he does hers to-night; and as he did Felice Charmond's last year; and Suke Damson's the year before!"

Revisions like this will doubtless recall to the minds of many readers Hardy's statement on one of the pages of *The Mayor of Casterbridge* that " 'Character is Fate,' said Novalis." Whatever may have been the fatalistic orientation of his earlier novels, by the time that Hardy came to write *The Mayor of Casterbridge* he had learned that the fault was not in Michael Henchard's stars but in himself that he was the failure he turned out to be. And in Hardy's successive attempts to clarify the character of Dr. Fitzpiers and to show what "a forlorn hope" was Grace's, we can observe the continuance, into the pages of *The Woodlanders,* of Novalis's thesis as an active influence in Hardy's mind. Nor is this all. Knowing, as we now know, that *The Woodlanders* was to be followed by *Tess* and *Jude the Obscure*—novels in which Fate (or God) and Character were to be replaced by Society as the chief cause of man's unhappy lot—knowing this, we can detect with profit the appearance of this idea in *The Woodlanders,* perhaps its very first appearance in any of the Wessex novels. In the next to the last chapter, Grace is described as taking down a prayer-book and turning to the marriage-service. "She became lost in long ponderings.... That particular sentence, beginning, 'whom God hath joined together,' was a staggerer for a gentle woman of strong devotional sentiment. She wondered whether God really did join them together." William R. Rutland has righly observed: "The interest of this does not lie in whether it is true . . . but in its being there at all. For it . . . strikes a note which is wholly new in Hardy's fiction. . . . His quarrel with human society for its attitude toward sexual relationships . . . is [here] inaugurated...."

A careful scrutinizing of Hardy's revisions during the quarter-century in which the definitive text of *The Woodlanders* was in the making will help to make clear that this novel stands in a pivotal position among Hardy's works. He began his career as a novelist with the peasant's stoic conviction that "your lot is your lot," as Henery Fray puts it in *Far from the Madding Crowd,* or that your troubles are "the fault of some indistinct, colossal Prince of the World who rules your lot," as Eustacia Vye puts it in *The Return of the Native.* Novalis helped Hardy to learn that human character had more to do with the production of misery than he had at first thought. But not until he had settled into Max Gate and had begun to enter more frequently and more intimately into "society" did Hardy come to a clear realization that man-made laws and conventions may play a large part in causing happiness or wretchedness. The pages of *The Woodlanders* mark the first dawning of the light—some would prefer to call it a blight—the first firing of the reformer's zeal, at any rate the first expression of the socially-conscious conviction which eventually (in 1922, in the "Apology" prefixed to *Late Lyrics)* enabled Hardy to opine that pain can "be kept down to a minimum by loving-kindness, operating through scientific knowledge, and actuated by the modicum of free will conjecturally possessed" by mankind when cosmic forces "happen to be in equilibrium."

The use, therefore, of Hardy's definitive text of *The Woodlanders* is not merely a matter of giving the reader access to the novelist's most polished phraseology; it is also a matter of letting him see most clearly into Hardy's thought and into his reading of character. By the time that he came to write *The Woodlanders,* Hardy was ready to embark upon the writing of his novels "with a purpose," and many of his revisions in the text were aimed at accomplishing his purpose more effectively. It is, therefore, all the more unfortunate that none of his efforts at clarification reached the thirty American editions of *The Woodlanders* printed between 1887 and 1926. It is, I think, significant that, in more recent years, American readers who are known to have had access to the London editions of the novel have been as ardent in their praise of *The Woodlanders* as the most enthusiastic British reader. A. Edward Newton, who owned a copy of the first edition, called *The Woodlanders* "one of the best novels of the last century." William Lyon Phelps selected this as "the most beautiful and most noble" of Hardy's novels. Professor Samuel C. Chew, who, before writing his excellent little monograph on Hardy, had informed himself about the definitive edition of 1912, called *The Woodlanders* "the most tender of all Hardy's books." But the large body of American readers have had to put up with one or another of the thirty lame ducks already noted. The presence, to this day, of so many defective American editions of this novel in libraries used by American teachers and scholars may have more than a little to do with the general neglect of *The Woodlanders* in academic circles. In spite of the high praise given to this novel, there are many teachers of Victorian fiction who confess to having never read it. There is no American annotated school-or-college edition of this novel. Whereas there are at least seven American textbook editions of *The Return of the Native*,[8] and four textbook editions of *The Mayor of Casterbridge*,[9] and two textbook editions of *Far from the Madding Crowd*,[10] and one annotated textbook edition of *Tess of the D'Urbervilles*,[11] *The Wood-*

[8] These are: 1, edited by John W. Cunliffe, in the Modern Students' Library (Scribners, 1917); 2, edited by Warner Taylor, in Harper's Modern Classics series (Harpers, 1922); 3, edited by A. C. Baugh, in Modern Readers' Series (Macmillan, 1928); 4, edited by Carl Van Doren, in the Guild Classics series (Literary Guild, 1931); 5, edited by Irene M. Haworth (Ginn and Company, 1931); 6, edited by Roger S. Loomis, in *Modern English Readings* (Farrar & Rinehart, 1934); 7, edited by James D. McCallum, in the *College Omnibus* (Harcourt, Brace, 1935).

[9] Edited by 1, J. F. A. Pyre, in Modern Classics series (Harpers, 1922); 2, Ernest F. Amy (Nelson, 1933); 3, James D. McCallum, in *College Omnibus* (Harcourt, Brace, 1933); 4, Harvey C. Webster (Rinehart, 1948).

[10] Edited by 1, William T. Brewster, in Modern Classics series (Harpers, 1918); 2, Carl J. Weber (Oxford University Press, New York, 1937; revised 1941; revised 1948).

[11] Edited with Notes by Carl J. Weber, in Harper's Modern Classics (Harper, 1935; 1940).

landers remains, like Marty South herself, alone, neglected, and ignored.[12]

Thomas Hardy died on January 11, 1928. On the following Sunday, January 15, the *Sunday Times* of London printed a number of obituary articles; among them was one by Newman Flower entitled "In his Wessex Home." From this article (page 12) I quote:

> *The Woodlanders*, he once told me, was his [Hardy's] favourite book, and he added: "I used to write it in portions once a week—on Fridays." It is almost incredible that such a masterpiece could be written from week to week in this manner, but the sheer genius of this man could do anything.

We now know that *The Woodlanders* as it stands in the definitive edition is the result of labor begun in 1885 and continued until 1912—a stretch of twenty-seven years. "The sheer genius of this man" could do many things, but it should now be clear that genius did not lead to Hardy's shirking the toil and the prolonged drudgery that went into polishing the style and strengthening the structure of his work. The result of his labor deserves far more attention than it has as yet received from American students. As the London *Athenaeum* once remarked of *The Woodlanders:* "It should be read by all who can tell masterly work in fiction when they see it."

A CHECK-LIST OF THE EDITIONS OF *The Woodlanders*

1. London, Macmillan & Co., 3 vols., first edition, March 15, 1887.
2. New York, Harper & Brothers, March 25, 1887; first American edition.
3. New York, Harpers, Franklin Square Library No. 572, March 25, 1887.
4. New York, George Munro, Seaside Library No. 957, April 16, 1887.
5. New York, Norman Munro, Munro's Library No. 725, April 30, 1887.

[12] I have annotated a few passages from *The Woodlanders* in an article in *ELH: a Journal of English Literary History*, II (1935), 242-245.

6. New York, John W. Lovell, Lovell's Library No. 956, May 7, 1887.
7. London, Macmillan, 1 vol., Macmillan's Colonial Library No. 49, 1887.
8. London, Macmillan, "Second Edition," August, 1887.
9. New York, George Munro, "Twenty-five cent editions," No. 114 (1887?).
10. London, Macmillan, 1889. Reprint of No. 8.
11. New York, United States Book Co. (1890? Listed in their 1890 catalogue; no copy seen by present compiler.)
12. New York, A. L. Burt, Manhattan Library No. 45, January 16 (1891?).
13. New York, Hovendon Co. (1892?).
14. New York, International Book Co., Fireside Series (1893?).
15. New York, A. L. Burt, Manhattan Library, New Series No. 109, May 11, 1895.
16. London, Osgood, McIlvaine & Co., 1896; with a Preface.
17. New York, Harpers, 1896. Reprint of No. 2.
18. Chicago, Rand, McNally; Globe Library No. 235, 1896.
19. New York, R. F. Fenno & Co., Lavender Series (1897?).
20. New York, George Munro's Sons, Royal Series No. 83, May 27, 1898.
21. New York, Hovendon Co. (1898?). Reprint of No. 13.
22. Chicago, Rand, McNally; Alpha Library, No.? (1899?).
23. New York, Harpers, "Wessex Edition," red cloth, gilt tops; 1900.
24. New York, Street & Smith, Arrow Library No. 230, 1901.
25. New York, Peter Fenelon Collier (1902?).
26. New York, American Publishers Corporation, Chelsea Series No. 146, n.d. (1902?)
27. New York, Fifth Avenue Publishing Co., n.d. Red lettering.
28. New York, Fifth Avenue Publishing Co., n.d. Maple-leaf edition.
29. London, Macmillan, 1903. Reprint of No. 16 (by a new publisher).
30. Chicago, Rand, McNally; Library Edition, red buckram, n.d.
31. New York, Harpers, 1905. Cheap green cloth; reprint of No. 23.
32. New York, Harpers, 1905. "Wessex Edition," colored title-page, bright green cloth.
33. New York, Harpers, n.d. Reprint of No. 31; "MCMV" removed from t-p.
34. London, Macmillan, Pocket Edition, 1906.
35. New York, Harpers, Thin-paper Edition, 1910.

36. London, Macmillan, "Wessex Edition," 1912.
37. New York, Harpers, "Autograph Edition," 1912; 153 copies.
38. London, Macmillan, 1913; reprint of No. 29.
39. London, Macmillan, 1916; reprint of No. 34.
40. New York, Harpers, 1917; reprint of No. 17.
41. London, Macmillan, 1920; reprint of No. 36.
42. London, Macmillan, "Mellstock Edition," 1920; 2 vols.
43. New York, Harpers, "Anniversary Edition," 1921.
44. London, Macmillan, 1924; reprint of No. 34.
45. New York, Harpers, 1926; reprint of No. 17.
46. New York, Harpers, 1928. Current "trade edition," new format, designed by Arthur Rushmore, using plates of No. 37; reprinted in 1930 and 1938.
47. New York, Harpers, Modern Classics Edition, 1932.
48. London, Macmillan, "Scholars' Library," 1934.
49. London, Macmillan, 1935; reprint of No. 48.
50. New York, Harpers, 1937; reprint of No. 47.

CARL J. WEBER

Colby College

VIII
Science in the Dramas of Henry Arthur Jones

HENRY ARTHUR JONES supported his crusade for the new drama with the effort to put the best thought of the late Victorian period on the stage and thus to bring the drama abreast of other literature. As the best thought included science, Jones created characters in terms of their heredity, employed numerous scientists as spokesmen in his dramas, and treated themes meditated in the light of his knowledge of science.

With no schooling after the age of twelve, Jones educated himself by reading that included "extensive foragings among the sciences."[1] His interest in drama and in science developed together. Eighteen when he first saw a play, Jones said, "I . . . gave most of my leisure to seeing plays and reading Herbert Spencer."[2] He would go without meals to buy theatre tickets and books. Writing to Emery Walker in 1878, he said:

I am still reading hard; all my spare time in the day and sometimes half the night. I am now approaching the end of Herbert Spencer's system of philosophy. It has been a hard nut to crack, but I wanted first of all to get a good groundwork of the latest science to build upon. And Herbert Spencer must not merely be read; he must be learned.[3]

[1] Doris Arthur Jones, *The Life and Letters of Henry Arthur Jones* (London, 1930), p. 31.
[2] *Ibid.*, p. 34.
[3] *Ibid.*, p. 39.

Throughout his life, Jones was "intensely interested in scientific subjects, especially natural science."[4] Cordell emphasizes Jones's reading of Spencer, Darwin, Huxley, and Butler.[5] The London production of *The Dancing Girl* quoted Spencer, who invited Jones to call. After their conversation, Doris Jones reports, "My father said constantly, 'Any clear thinking I've done I owe to Herbert Spencer.'"[6]

Jones's views were strongly influenced by this reading. The opening word in the Preface of his *The Foundations of a National Drama* is "Huxley," and the opening sentiment paraphrases Huxley's prayer that fortune give him courage to speak the truth.[7] His speeches are sprinkled with references to scientific conclusions. He came to believe in "great changeless laws and principles . . . everywhere and always in operation, that irresistibly rule men with an iron compulsion."[8] This concept is evident in the famous line in Jones's early melodrama, *The Silver King* (1882): "O God! put back Thy universe and give me yesterday!"[9] One is reminded of Wells's "The Man Who Could Work Miracles," in which stopping time for a moment wrecks the world.

But Jones's views from scientific reading were curiously mixed with many attitudes of mid-Victorian conservatism. Cordell says that Jones "was a Tory in politics . . . an honest proponent of the double standard of morality, a foe of women's suffrage, popular education, Irish independence, and experimental social legislation."[10] To the extent that nineteenth-century science implied a new morality, Jones drew back from it.

Jones began his play-writing with stock pieces like *It's Only*

---

[4] *Ibid.*, p. 40.
[5] Richard A. Cordell, *Henry Arthur Jones and the Modern Drama* (New York, 1932), p. 22.
[6] *Op. cit.*, p. 114.
[7] (New York and London, 1912), p. vii.
[8] Henry Arthur Jones, *My Dear Wells* (London, 1921, 2nd edition), p. 259.
[9] In Clayton Hamilton, ed., *Representative Plays by Henry Arthur Jones* (Boston, 1925), I, Act II, Scene iv.
[10] *Op. cit.*, p. 67.

Round the Corner (1878) and *Hearts of Oak* (1879). But melodrama no longer serves, he wrote in 1891, because "The piercing light of science has been sprung upon us behind the scenes, and our old worn-out apparatus of theatrical effect and situation looks half ghastly, half trumpery in that cold cruel beam."[11] The drama must express the thought of the age, religious, political, and especially scientific.[12] His early melodramas treat the lower classes sympathetically; *The Middleman* (1889), Cordell notes, displays "a sympathy with the worker that contrasts noticeably with . . . [the] reactionary attitude of later years."[13] Apparently under the influence of both Ibsen and science, Jones meditated some naturalistic plays to treat heredity, environment, and social responsibility: a play to be named *Coleridge,* concerned with heredity and madness; a play to deal with "The physical basis of all mental states and the relation of character to brain formation"; and a play to be named *Doctor Irving* concerned with inherited diseases.[14] But conservatism triumphed, and Jones turned his back upon the subjects of the Ibsen-school. By 1891, he was protesting against "modern realism which founded dramas on disease, ugliness, and vice."[15] Though expressing admiration for Ibsen's "imaginative side,"[16] he stated that "Ibsen had nothing whatever to do" with *Judah* and added that, "I must not render to him what is due in *Judah* to Huxley."[17] Jones came to rest in the ideas of Spencer, Arnold, Ruskin, and Huxley.[18] When the drama came to treat radical ideas more favorably than he wished, Jones spoke of the immeasurably higher function of drama to interpret life, to encourage a "broad, sane, and profound morality."[19] His later plays treat the moral

[11] Preface to *Saints and Sinners* (London and New York, 1891), p. x.
[12] Cordell, *op. cit.,* p. 63.
[13] *Ibid.,* p. 49.
[14] *Ibid.,* pp. 64-65.
[15] Doris Arthur Jones, *op. cit.,* p. 88.
[16] *Ibid.,* p. 88.
[17] Cordell, *op. cit.,* p. 81.
[18] *Ibid.,* p. 54.
[19] Henry Arthur Jones, "A Lecture Delivered at the Royal Institution" (March 18, 1904), in *The Foundations of a National Drama, op. cit.,* p. 17.

problems of the upper classes, and at last, though he did not abandon the serious drama altogether, he did his best writing in high comedy.

Jones did not need science in his high comedies. Though scientists and their points of view appear after 1900 (for instance, in *The Galilean's Victory*, 1907), science is found in Jones's plays chiefly in the period of transition, from *The Middleman* in 1889 through *The Physician* in 1897. In this period, Jones created many characters in terms of science, especially the factor of heredity. At the same time, he sought to use his characters as spokesmen for various points of view, to "shoot his own philosophy of life and views of men and the world through them."[20] Some characters, especially men of science, are spokesmen for advanced views, attitudes, or ideas that Jones did not agree with. His disagreement leads, in some plays, to confused conclusions.

Jones's first use of heredity is mechanical and obvious. In *The Silver King* (1882) it is necessary in the plot that the hero, Denver, appear as a drunkard; it is also necessary that the audience sympathize with him. To gain this sympathy, Jones has Jaikes explain that Denver inherited a tendency to drink:

Bless you, it's the blood; he's got too much nature in him, that's where it is. His father was just like him when he was a young man.... And his grandfather, old Squire Denver, just such another. There was a man for you if you like. The last ten years of his life he never went to bed sober one night.[21]

Slightly more subtle use of heredity appears in *Saints and Sinners* (1884). Captain Eustace Fanshawe, an avowed villain, has just a touch of decency in his nature. He says to the audience in a soliloquy:

I might have been a good man, I suppose,—if I could have chosen my own father and mother, and if everything and every creature I've met, from my cradle upwards, hadn't pushed me to the bad.[22]

[20] Henry Arthur Jones, "The Drama and Real Life" (November 13, 1897), *ibid.*, p. 143.
[21] Act I, Scene i.
[22] Act II, Scene i.

Apparently Jones was seeking to tint the blackness of his villain, or perhaps indirectly to highlight the use of heredity in the treatment of the heroine, Letty, seduced by Fanshawe. To gain sympathy for her, Jones traces her weakness to a bad strain in her blood. She is like her mother's people.

LYDIA. . . . she favours the Langtons, her mother's family. The Langtons was Church folk, and always very gay and worldly.
LOT. Ah, didn't one of the Miss Langtons—
LYDIA. Yes, but that ain't neither here nor there. Miss Letty it was, that's her picture. . . . Our miss Letty is named after her.[23]

When Letty shows signs of loving pleasure, her father Jacob says to himself: "How like she grows to her aunt." When he hears of her association with Captain Fanshawe, he tells Letty the history of her aunt:

You asked me for your aunt Letty's history just now. Look at that picture; she was once as happy and as lovely and innocent as you are now. A few years and she came back to die in our arms, her heart broken, her beauty and innocence gone.[24]

After Letty has run away with Fanshawe, Jacob forgives her, realizing, as he makes clear by a pointed action, that the cause for Letty's weakness is a taint of blood: He "takes up LETTY's old garden hat, puts it down, happens to see picture of LETTY's aunt, goes to it, turns its face to the wall."[25]

The Middleman (1889) advances from this excusatory use of heredity to presentation of the traits of a father reflected in two daughters. The daughters are temperamentally different, but both Mary and Nancy are credibly daughters of Cyrus Blenkarn. Cyrus is especially fond of Mary, because she shares his spiritual qualities. Like Cyrus, Mary is absent-minded, impractical, dreamy. Mary does not care whether Cyrus wears a coat and tie, any more than Cyrus does, but she is lovingly interested in his work. Like Cyrus, she is secretive; she suffers in silence without

[23] Act I.
[24] Act I.
[25] Act II, Scene iii.

resentment. "I'm quite well!" she says when she is noticeably ill; "How have the new vases turned out?" "There's nobody in the world understands me but you, dear!" says Cyrus.[26] Mary exhibits the quixotic pride characteristic of her father; when Chandler offers her more than her wages, though Mary needs money desperately, she takes exactly what is due, "Not a farthing more." When Chandler asks her not to mention the name of his son as her seducer, Mary is almost insulted: "Do you think it possible I could?" she says.[27]

Nancy is the practical daughter, reflecting the streak in Cyrus that is manifest when he sets himself to ruin Chandler. She exhibits the traits of the daughter who has had to perform the daily chores and settle the little bills, for a number of years.

The study of heredity goes deeper in *Judah*. Judah is religiously fanatic and mystically poetic. Jones indicates these conflicting traits in the name, Judah Llewellyn, and he calls attention to them in the lines of the play. Papworthy says Judah's eloquence is not education, ". . . it's born in him!" "Welsh, isn't he?" says the scientist Jopp.

PAPWORTHY. A Welsh father and a Jewish mother.
JOPP. Celt and Jew! Two good races! Just the man to give England a new religion, or make her believe in her old one.[28]

The dramatic struggle that takes place within Judah is a struggle between Hebraic rigidity of conscience and loyalty to an idealized love.

Judah's antagonist is Jopp the scientist, who has no faith in anything not apparent to reason or demonstrable in the laboratory. He is, however, human, willing to admire sincerity in Judah and finally even to forgive Judah and Vashti, though not her rascally father. Jopp's daughter, however, inherits the rationalism of her father in an unmitigated form: exhibiting

---

[26] In Hamilton, ed., *op. cit.*, I, Act I.
[27] Act II.
[28] In Hamilton, ed., *op. cit.*, I, Act I.

Jopp's temperament plus the new feminism of her time, she is a caricature of the suffragette brought up in a laboratory.

The hereditary relationships of even the minor characters are studied in this play, Jones's first play belonging to the new drama with little of the old melodrama about it. Juxon Prall, Sophie's young man, may not seem at first glance the son of his father and mother. Mr. and Mrs. Prall are literary; they are simple-minded, credulous, egotistic, and argumentative. Prall is so fatuous and credulous that Juxon, equally argumentative and educated in the new schools, has tried to convert him to reason. The resulting arguments, along with Juxon's admiration of Sophie, have driven Juxon into belligerent rationalism. That he is none the less the son of his father is pointed out in the irony in one of Juxon's speeches. "How strange it is," says Sophie, "that people like your parents should possess such a gifted son as you!" With inherited egotism, Juxon replies: "It is one of the freaks of heredity. My brother James is not gifted. When I think of poor James, I am ashamed of my attainments."[29] He speaks later of the "infirmity of those who by some curious stroke of irony stand to me in the relation of father and mother." Jones's stroke of irony is that Juxon is a chip off the old block, after all.[30]

Jones again presents a study of heredity as a basis for dramatic conflict in *Michael and His Lost Angel* (1896). As in *Judah*, the protagonist is a man divided against himself. The conflicting elements in Michael are a mystic Puritanism inherited from his mother and a strain of the "old Adam" inherited from his father.

---

[29] Act II.

[30] Even Lady Eve, motherless and dying of the weakness that took her brothers and sisters, exhibits a study in heredity. Her father's solicitous pity for her and his concern with the extinction of his family are reflected in her own attraction to death. He says, "My dear one! My only one! The last of us! The end of our race! . . . I have followed six of them to the grave, one after another, and now this last one is to be taken." And she says: "How sweet Death seems sometimes! Like a kiss from an unknown lover! He comes and touches you and says, 'Don't you know me? I have loved you all these years. This is our wedding-day. You must come with me.'" (Act I.)

Michael inherited his religiosity, combining Puritanism and mysticism, from his dead mother, whose brother, a Catholic priest, is the living representative of this element. "My mother was a deeply religious woman," says Michael, "and before my birth she consecrated me to this service as Hannah consecrated Samuel. When she was dying she said to me, 'I'm not leaving you. I shall watch over you every moment of your life.' "[31] Michael has idealized his mother all his life. He speaks of her as if she were alive; he converses with her portrait. This portrait is a "painting of a lady about twenty-eight, very delicate and spirituelle." Michael in turn has an "ascetic, scholarly face, with much sweetness and spirituality of expression."[32] Michael always says his prayers before this portrait. Its influence upon him may be seen in his Eastern studies, translations from the Arabic, the composition of an exalted book called *The Hidden Life,* and lonely devotions on Saint Decuman's Island. When sin drives him to seek a deeper peace, a more absolute submission of the will to God, Michael turns to his mother's brother.

How could this man, consecrated in heart and mind, son of a woman idealized as an angel, and rigidly Puritanical in his insistence that Rose Gibbard publicly confess her sin, fall prey to an adventuress like Audrie? Michael is also the son of his father, Sir Lyolf Feversham, a good man, but worldly, tolerant, slightly sceptical, prepared to accept Michael's doctrines and to go all lengths with Michael, "on condition," he says, "that I indulge the latent old Adam in me with an occasional mild joke at his expense."[33] There is just enough of this "old Adam" in Michael to explain his fall and his later statement "No,"[34] he is not sorry. In one other subtle trait, Michael reflects his father's temperament, a streak of fatalism. "Love is love," says Sir Lyolf, "and whether it comes from heaven, or whether it comes from the other place, there's no escaping it."[35] Michael analyzes how there was no escaping the "hundred little chances, accidents as

[31] In Hamilton, ed., *op. cit.*, III, Act I.
[32] Act I. [33] Act I. [34] Act III. [35] Act V.

well call them, that gave us to each other," till Audrie rebukes this fatalism with: "It's no use blaming chance or fate, or whatever it is."[86] Sir Lyolf's only rôle in the drama is to exhibit the hereditary explanation for Michael's fall.

Audrie is likewise complex and likewise the victim of heredity. Her character is shot through with a streak of mockery and defiance of convention. This streak seems one she would like to deny, but cannot because it is a part of her. Even at the point of death, as she looks forward to meeting Michael again in Heaven, she expresses a half-sceptical witticism, and her dying words are: "Oh! don't look so solemn—"[87] Though her parents do not appear, Mark Docwray tells enough of her background to explain this streak. "She was the only daughter," he says, "of an Australian millionaire. Her great-grandfather, I believe, was an Australian convict."[88] There is no reason for Jones to have invented these lines except to explain Audrie's character.[39]

In *The Physician* (1897) Edana and her father, Reverend Peregrine Hinde, are credibly father and daughter. Edana is an idealist-ingénue in white muslin; her father poses as a male "ingénu," blending, as he says, the "transparent innocence of the dove with the subtle and useful wisdom of the serpent."[40] Dr. Carey refuses to keep Amphiel's dipsomania a secret from Edana because, he tells Amphiel, she might marry him and bear children who "will perhaps inherit your taint in every bone and nerve."[41]

The Goal (1897) not only traces heredity through three generations, but presents a lecture on eugenics. At the point of

[36] Act III.
[37] Act V.
[38] Act I.
[39] Rose, in the same play, is credibly the daughter of Andrew Gibbard; they react to shame in the same quietly tortured way; they react to Michael's confession with the same covert sympathy. Andrew says, however, that Rose is like her dead mother, an item that deepens Andrew's pain at her confession: "a little twitch of her lip like her mother used to have... I couldn't bear it any longer." (Act I.)
[40] (London and New York, 1899), Act III.
[41] Act III.

death, Sir Stephen tells his physician that, before starting in life, he took the "one great step to secure success and happiness. . . . I made," he says, "an excellent choice of my father and mother. . . . good, sound, healthy stock on both sides."[42] The qualities inherited from this sound stock, Sir Stephen passed on to his son Dan. Father and son are both robust, stubborn, quarrelsome, and in love with their creative work as engineers. "I've done very well," boasts Dan. "Of course you have," says Sir Stephen. "You're my son."

When pretty Peggie Lovel comes in from next door, Sir Stephen lectures her on the choice of a husband:

Be sure that he has a good full open eye that can look you straight in the face. . . . Take care he hasn't got a queer-shaped head, or a low forehead. A good round head, and a good full high forehead. . . . Don't say "Yes" till you've seen him out of trousers, in riding dress, or court dress. . . . a good, well-shaped leg, eh, Peggie? . . . doesn't squint, doesn't stammer; hasn't got any nervous tricks or twitchings.[43]

In *The Galilean's Victory* (1907), Fyson, the grandfather-scientist, Christabel, his daughter, and Ione, his grandchild, share traits of temperament. Fyson is sceptical, easy-going in most matters, but devoted to his scientific work. Christabel, though married to the scientist Nuneham and in love with the physician Rex Allen, finds a hobby in religion. She has tried three, Welsh Congregationalism, Roman Catholicism, and Anglicanism, and is toying with a fourth, Rebbings's brand of Christian Socialism. But she is still a sceptical and restless woman, in need of something to absorb her energies as science absorbs those of her father and her husband. Her child, Ione, has the mother's playfulness and imagination, the energy of both mother and grandfather. In the same play, Fyson playfully discusses heredity with Ben and Sally Possiter, father and daughter from the lower class—a stupid, vicious pair, who boast of their

[42] In Hamilton, ed., *op. cit.*, IV, 310 (a one-act play).
[43] *Ibid.*, p. 318.

wickedness as a family trait. The latest scientific researches in heredity, says Fyson, indicate that we are no longer able to saddle our misdeeds upon our ancestors. "That's a pity, dear gentleman!" says Ben Possiter, and Fyson agrees, "A great pity. ... I don't like the prospect!"[44]

Men of science in Jones's plays are widely different, but alike in traits that we may regard as representing Jones's concept of a man of science. In 1889, the year *The Middleman* was produced and not long before *Judah*, Jones said:

> When. . . this age and its works can be dispassionately . . . weighed, who can doubt that its prime achievements, its crowning glories, its great prizes will be adjudged to science? . . .
> But on the stage on such rare occasions as the man of science is introduced, it is always. . . as a weak-minded, insincere, comic old fool. . . with an entirely false, ridiculous jargon, and generally with a very strong dash of the impostor.[45]

When he turned to the presentation of scientists, therefore, Jones sought to present credible portraits, even when his intention was also to satirize the scientist.

Critics do not agree that Jones altogether succeeded. A. B. Walkley almost at once scored Jones's portrait of Cyrus Blenkarn in *The Middleman* as unrealistic:

> We all know [he said] the type of modern inventor—a Pasteur, an Eiffel, an Edison. Has Mr. Jones tried to realize this type for us on the stage? Not a bit of it. His inventor is of the old, old footlight

---

[44] (London, 1907), Act II. (Produced as *The Evangelist*.) The fact that Jones was not a social reformer and did not believe that a changed environment would change human nature may account for his failure to stress environment as a factor in character. In *Judah*, however, he included some environmental factors. Judah's temperament is presented as a resultant, in part, of his solitary childhood, keeping his father's sheep on the hills in Wales. "You know I lived almost alone," he says, "until I was nearly twenty. I saw no human being, sometimes spoke to no one, from one week to another." (Act I.) In the next Act, he says: "Till six years ago I never had any companions but the hills and my father's cattle." Perhaps Lady Eve's self-pity is due as much to her father's indulgent love as to anything she inherited.

[45] "The First-Night Judgment of Plays," *Nineteenth Century Review* (July, 1889), in *The Renascence of the English Drama* (London, 1895), p. 60.

sort: an unpractical, dazed, almost demented dreamer. . . . Such inventors. . . are not the typical inventors of today.[46]

There is truth in Walkley's observation. But in 1889, Jones was still feeling his way out of the melodrama. Even so, Cordell suggests that Jones was not merely throwing an old stereotype on the stage. The most eccentric action in the play had a basis in "the story of Bernard Palissy, who is said to have used his furniture for fuel when he was inventing the ware which now goes by his name."[47] As Cordell says, Dr. Carey of *The Physician* "belongs to Bohemia's crowded seacoast and not to Harley Street,"[48] but then the whole play is "old and tawdry,"[49] a throwback for 1897. Sometimes pictures that look like caricatures to twentieth-century eyes may not be so. When a critic called Professor Sturgess of *Dolly Reforming Herself* a caricature, Jones replied, "I think Professor Sturgess must be accepted. I gave him the humorless, portentous manner of Herbert Spencer."[50]

Jones's men of science are usually described in stage directions and elsewhere as studious, methodical, aloof, objective, intellectual, and sceptical. The first important scientist, besides Cyrus Blenkarn, is Professor Jopp of *Judah*, a research-worker in biology and author of articles like "The Scientific Conception of Truth." He is "keen, alert, intellectual; bald, very high forehead, bright deep-set eyes, genial Voltaire type of face."[51] David Remon, the astronomer of *The Masqueraders*, is "pale, studious, philosophic-looking."[52] Dr. Carey of *The Physician* has "a strong intellectual face; sensitive mobile features, with frequently changing play of humour and melancholy."[53] Philip

[46] *Playhouse Impressions* (London, 1892), p. 117.
[47] *Op. cit.*, p. 47.
[48] *Ibid.*, p. 130.
[49] Allardyce Nicoll, *A History of Late Nineteenth Century Drama 1850-1900* (Cambridge, 1946), I, 167.
[50] Cordell, *op. cit.*, pp. 233-234.
[51] Act I.
[52] In Hamilton, ed., *op. cit.*, II, Act I.
[53] Act I.

Nuneham of *The Galilean's Victory*, mineralogist and chemist, is "calm, well-bred, thoughtful, with a quiet, dispassionate, but not unkind, manner. . . . a strong-minded, fair-minded, entirely truthful and sincere man—withal a little cold and dull."[54] Jones's portrait of Herbert Spencer, Professor Sturgess of *Dolly Reforming Herself*, is a psychologist, a "hard, dry, narrow, fattish scientific man."[55] As the play develops, he is seen to be slightly eccentric, self-centered, and mechanically regular in all his routines. A few of Jones's scientists are so eccentric that other people look upon them as mad. The innkeeper Brinkler speaks of David Remon of *The Masqueraders* as: "That mad gentleman that lives at Gerard's Heath,"[56] and when David's brother and understudy, Eddie, enters, he is described as "highly refined, overstrung, unbalanced."[57]

Eccentricity is exhibited in absent-mindedness, unworldliness, and impracticality. Cyrus Blenkarn of *The Middleman* is a type belonging to melodrama: he comes to a reception in his shirt-sleeves without a tie; he can hardly remember whether he ate dinner and supposes he ate his favorite Irish stew instead of veal pie. He has no idea what happens to his money: "What would it matter to *me* if I had all the money in the world so long as I couldn't turn out a bit of work like that!"[58] When, finally successful, he is invited to dine with Sir Seton and Lady Umfraville, he refuses because, "I've had to work all my life, and I can't begin to play now."[59] David Remon of *The Masqueraders* is no longer the caricature of melodrama, but he exhibits the same unworldliness refined to philosophic detachment: "Is anything real?" he says. "I've lived so long alone with only Eddie that the world has grown quite spectral to me."[60] This unworldliness goes along with scorn for Philistine values. Jesse Pegg tries to tell Cyrus of *The Middleman* that his invention created the Tatlow porcelain works, put Tatlow on the map, and made the

---

[54] Act I.
[55] In Hamilton, ed., *op. cit.*, IV, Act I.
[56] Act I.   [57] Act I.   [58] Act II.   [59] Act IV.   [60] Act I.

capitalist Joseph Chandler "an ornament, a glory, and a bulwark to the British nation"—at Cyrus's expense, because Cyrus would not pay attention to money. "Yes, I know, Jesse," says Cyrus, "but you're wasting my time."[61] When, however, Chandler's son brings shame to Mary, Cyrus realizes his folly, but rails at the standards of the world:

My invention, the fruit of my brain, fed it [the town of Tatlow], and clothed it, and brought it to prosperity! . . . I suppose I am mad! I haven't fattened myself on another man's labour and tears! . . . God made this world for parasites![62]

David Remon of *The Masqueraders* scorns worldly values with an embittered irony. He has been trying to solve the mystery of sun-spots, and when asked the practical value of his researches, says:

Who solves the mystery of sun-spots may show the way to control the future harvests of the world; and who controls the harvests of the world will provide cheaper swipes and smaller beer for Brinkler's grandchildren.[63]

Scorn for Philistine values frequently merges into a cynical pessimism. Professor Jopp of *Judah* meets Prall's credulity with this statement:

My dear Prall, I've lived sixty years in this world. I have never met with a single instance of cheating or deception or fraud of any description. . . . no amount of evidence that my eyes or ears can bring shall ever shake my theory that human nature is absolutely above suspicion.[64]

When Sophie says it will be a satisfaction to expose Vashti and lock her up, Jopp says, "It's the British public that ought to be locked up till it learns wisdom."[65] In *The Masqueraders*, young Eddie Remon reflects David's ironic pessimism: "This is the very worst world that ever spun round, for a man who has a heart. Look at all the heartless and stupid people. . . . Oh, Davy, isn't there one perfect world out of all the millions?" David re-

[61] Act II.   [62] Act II.   [63] Act I.   [64] Act II.   [65] Act II.

plies, "There isn't one, Eddie, not one of all the millions."[66] Copeland, David's friend, goes off to climb mountains in Alaska, because, he says, "I'm sick of this nineteenth-century civilisation. I must do a bit of climbing, and get myself re-oxidised."[67] The Devil in *The Tempter*, who exhibits a good deal of scientific knowledge, expresses a similar cynical pessimism:

> ... man's an odd animal,
> Much lower than the angels; rather higher
> Than the brutes; false, envious, vicious, greedy,
> Ignorant, vain, inconstant, superstitious,
> Purposeless, impotent, ridiculous.
> ....
> He bribes his fellow-apes to flatter him,
> Sniffs up the incense of their mean applause,
> And calls it glory.[68]

Several of Jones's scientists take refuge in a playful, embittered fantasy. "After all," says Professor Jopp of *Judah*, "why not believe in fairy tales? Why not pretend there is a dryad in every tree, and a nymph in every brook?"[69] Dulcie in *The Masqueraders* amuses herself by making David play the fool. David, conscious of his rôle, says, "In a world of shadows, what does it matter what part one plays?"[70] He picks up Eddie's fantasy that there is a perfect world in the nebula of Andromeda and develops it in talking with Dulcie after her unhappy marriage:

Your trouble isn't real. This society world of yours isn't a real world. There's one little star in Andromeda where everything is real. You've wandered down here amongst these shadows when you should have stayed at home. . . . Fly back to Andromeda, and you will see what a dream all this is. . . . the little star in Andromeda is my home. I'm only wandering with you amongst these phantoms.[71]

Jones's scientists find in their work an absorbing refuge from the world. Cyrus Blenkarn of *The Middleman* exhibits a caricature of a scientist's fanatical absorption in his work. He comes

[66] Act I.   [67] Act I.
[68] In Hamilton, ed., *op. cit.*, II, Act I, Scene ii.
[69] Act III.   [70] Act I.   [71] Act II.

to a reception on a holiday pleading for materials; told to wait until tomorrow, he fumes: "I can't afford to waste any more time. I've wasted so many years already."[72] He is irritated that visitors come to his laboratory and tells them: "If you'll come some other day when I'm not busy—in about six months' time—or a year.... So proud I've seen you, so proud. Good morning!"[73] David Remon of *The Masqueraders* is torn between love and work. Dulcie tells him he must not go away to Africa, and at first he says that the mission to Africa will "crown all my life's work ... if it kills me, I must go.... I must be at my post, especially as it is a little dangerous."[74] In *The Physician*, Dr. Carey has come to a cynical belief in nothing. He says he does not even believe in his work, but he dreams, none the less, of going to India to work on cholera, and when he retires from Harley Street to the village of Fontleas, he sets up a laboratory in the bay of his living-room. When Dr. Brooker objects that he is wasting himself in Fontleas, Carey says: "Wasting myself! I work from morning to night.... Don't whisper it, Brooker, I fancy I'm on the track of the cancer microbe."[75] In *The Goal*, Sir Stephen Famariss is dying. The theme of the play is the vitality of this man, who dies as he has lived, with eager interest in his work. As he glances back at his busy life, recalling his "seventy-five glorious summers," the high spot is: "Eighty-four! I was boring a hole through the Rockies that summer—"[76] When his son Dan arrives, the talk is of work unfinished: "I want you to carry this Milford Haven scheme out! I want it to be said that what old Stephen Famariss couldn't do, young Dan Famariss could! ... Look here, you must start on this side. I've had all the soundings made—"[77] In *The Galilean's Victory*, heading a firm of engineers has not kept Philip Nuneham busy; he has taken up mineralogy and chemistry as a hobby and become absorbed in them. After a long evening, he tells his

[72] Act I. [73] Act II. [74] Act III. [75] Act III.
[76] *Op. cit.*, p. 311. [77] *Ibid.*

daughter, "Tell mamma I'm working, and I shall be very late," as he goes upstairs to his laboratory.[78]

Jones's men of science have an exalted sense of integrity in their work. When David Remon of *The Masqueraders*, for love of Dulcie, wavers in his decision to go to Africa, his little brother Eddie shames him: "Davy, you aren't going to sell them all like a—like a—They'll call you a—well, you fill in the word."[79] *The Masqueraders* is misunderstood if it is thought that David leaves Dulcie merely to preserve the letter of her marriage vows. The dramatically critical appeal is Helen's, to his conscience, but this appeal only tips the balance. David's wedding Dulcie with his mother's ring before he leaves suggests that he considers of little value Helen's moral that Dulcie is still Sir Brice's wife. Dr. Carey in *The Physician* struggles between hatred of the dipsomaniac Amphiel and his scientific integrity. "I hate him!" he tells Dr. Brooker. "Damn him! I hate him! for he stands between her and me. . . . but I want to save him. I began to feel proud of the case."[80] Scientific integrity wins; he does all he can for Amphiel. In *The Galilean's Victory*, Christabel's lover, the villain of the piece, is Dr. Rex Allen. He abandoned his post in West Africa for Christabel's sake, and he is defiant in his love for her until he learns that his partner died. Then remorse overcomes him: "Poor Dick! . . . I left him to die. I left my post, and came home to bring misery here! What a scoundrel I've been!"[81] The major struggle in *The Knife* (1909) concerns the integrity of Sir Mark Ridgeway as a surgeon. He discovers his wife's infidelity just before he operates on her lover, Kingsford. The slightest slip of the knife would dispose of Kingsford. The wife and Kingsford take it for granted that Kingsford will be murdered, but there is no question in Sir Mark's mind: the operation is successful.

Yet scientific work, absorbing as it is, is not enough to fill the lives of all Jones's scientists. For a little while, David Remon of *The Masqueraders* wavers; he turns his back upon his work.

[78] Act II.   [79] Act IV.   [80] Act III.   [81] Act IV.

This journey to Africa—it was the object of my life—it's less than nothing to me now. . . . I've made the one great discovery there was to make. . . . We astronomers have been puzzling all our lives to find out what gravitation is. I've found it out. Gravitation is love.[82]

He reflects that "Perhaps I've played the great game of life like a fool. . . . Right—wrong—duty—they may be all shadows, but my love for you is real." None the less, at the end of this speech, he turns again to his work. "Kiss me once—I've held you sacred! . . . Good bye. No, stay. . . . Drink with me. . . . Now Eddie, our work!"[83] The same conflict has a somewhat different outcome in *The Physician*. When the play opens, Dr. Carey is overworked to the point of breakdown, or at least what he calls, "Middle age. Disillusionment. My youth's gone. My beliefs are gone. I enjoy nothing. I believe in nothing," even, "My work means nothing to me." None the less, he tells Lady Valerie that he proposes to spend the "thirty good years of life in front of me. . . . In work. In duty. . . . I should like to go to India and thoroughly work out these cholera experiments."[84] When he gets out into the country and falls in love with Edana, he plunges into research, it is true, but at the end of the play he gives up going to India: "I go to India, unless—unless—" and the curtain falls as she goes to him, presumably to keep him at home, if not out of the laboratory.

After the scientist is married, his devotion to science is likely to make him neglect his wife. Christabel Nuneham of *The Galilean's Victory* rationalizes that her husband does not care what she does: "He's absorbed in his scientific experiments, and doesn't trouble much about anything else."[85] Philip Nuneham, even before he discovers her infidelity, admits that he has neglected her: "I became more and more absorbed in my minerals and chemistry. . . . So we gradually settled down peaceably into our separate ruts."[86] When he does make the discovery, he reflects that "Science is the only faithful wife,"[87] and turns again

[82] Act IV. [83] Act IV. [84] Act I. [85] Act I.
[86] Act II. [87] Act IV.

to his laboratory. In *Dolly Reforming Herself,* Renie says: "After all, your husband isn't a machine."[88] Sir Mark in *The Knife* reflects concerning his wife: "I've often thought it was wrong of me to marry her, especially as I was already married to my work."[89]

Many of the ethical ideas expressed in the plays are based upon the reasoning of science. Among the earliest is a rationalization of wickedness. In the melodrama *The Silver King* the villain is a gentleman-burglar, the educated leader of a band of robbers. When his wife objects to his way of life, he says: "My dear Olive, all living creatures prey upon one another. The duck gobbles up the worm, the man gobbles up the duck, and then the worm gobbles up the man again. It's the great law of nature. My profession is just as good as any other, till I'm found out."[90]

But a knowledge of science is generally associated with high-minded, generous, or liberal views. Professor Jopp in *Judah* has a strong hatred of fraud. He threatens to send Vashti to jail if he discovers her to be playing tricks: "You're playing upon sacred feelings," he says; "and I warn you I shall be merciless to you."[91] But at last he is merciful toward all except the scoundrel Dethic. The astronomer David Remon in *The Masqueraders* has an exalted opinion of womanhood: "I've always kept my reverence for them, and I've always known that some day or the other I should meet one who would make me worship her." In the face of the fact that Dulcie is marrying for money, David refuses Copeland's fortune. "Thanks, George," he says; "I won't buy her."[92] He also has a strong feeling for such of the older verities as mother's love: "It's the one thing that shows what a sham the rest of the world is. That little star in Andromeda is

[88] In Hamilton, ed., *op. cit.,* IV, Act I.
[89] In Walter Prichard Eaton, ed., *One-Act Plays for Stage and Study* (New York and London: Samuel French, 1925, a one-act play).
[90] Act III, Scene i.   [91] Act II.   [92] Act I.

crowded with mothers."[93] Science has taught Philip Nuneham "duty to society," the religion of being "quite faithful to our fellow-men."[94]

Men of science everywhere in Jones's plays stand for reason; they are enemies of fraud and of phenomena that cannot be explained scientifically. The play *Judah* is largely concerned with the exposure of trickery posing as psychic phenomena. Cordell calls the scientist Jopp of this play a "scientific realist . . . suggested by Herbert Spencer."[95] Jopp makes a hobby of exposing spiritualists. He does not believe in miracles at home or those "that do not happen either in a remote century or a remote country."[96] He does not deny miracles; he explains, "The perfectly natural means by which miracles are always accomplished." Judah asks him what his last lecture was about:

JOPP. My last lecture was on tadpoles and lizards.
JUDAH. Mine was on the unseen world.
JOPP. [Dryly.] Ah! there I can't follow you.[97]

When Jopp meets Dethic he classifies him at once as: "genus, cheat; species, religious; variety, bogus-miracle business." A little later, ribbing Dethic, Jopp says:

I have in my little collection at home the liver-wing of a phoenix, the entire skeleton of a griffin in excellent preservation, and the only known specimen of the horn of a unicorn, but I have never met with anyone possessed of supernatural powers.[98]

When it is explained that Vashti must fast to gain strength for her miracles, Jopp says: "I don't quite follow the operation. So far from giving strength, any lengthened period of fasting must weaken."[99]

Jones's scientists are determinists. In the "Prologue" of *The Tempter*, Jones states his own determinism:

[93] Act II.   [94] Act IV.   [95] *Op. cit.*, p. 77.   [96] Act I.
[97] Act I.   [98] Act I.   [99] Act I.

> And we are pilgrims, shadowed on our way,
> Waging the old inexplicable strife
> With darkness, taint of blood, necessity,
> Fate, chance, or—what?

The Devil, exhibiting a knowledge of science, stands at the door of Canterbury Cathedral and, expressing a similar determinism, shouts at God:

> And Thou! Work out Thy cunning, aimless scheme;
> Spin round Thy maddening maze of foolish worlds
> . . . .
> Give Thou no hint wherefore Thou hast designed
> This deftly dovetailed chaos of creation
> To issues of stupendous nothingness![100]

Dolly Reforming Herself concerns whether Dolly Telfer can keep a resolution. Professor Sturgess does not think she can. Author of books called *Man, the Automaton* and *Free Will, the Illusion,* he believes that "free will is a purely subjective illusion" and that actions are "entirely dependent upon the condition, quantity and arrangement of certain atoms in the gray matter."[101] He exhibits pictures of criminals and points out that they were foredoomed to criminal lives by the shapes of their heads. On the other hand, when his wife carries on a flirtation, he blames her, as "in the present low moral and intellectual condition of the herd of mankind, free will is a plausible working hypothesis."[102] In the action of the play, Sturgess is right; Dolly is not able to keep her resolutions.

Jones's plays contain a good deal about religion, much of it stated through his men of science. The Bible-quoting hypocrites of *Saints and Sinners* in 1884 roused a storm of protest. Jones answered his critics in various ways, including the articles "Religion and the Stage" in January, 1885, and "The Bible on the Stage" in 1893. He challenged: "Has, then, this religion of yours grown so valetudinarian that . . . you must shelter it from the

[100] Act IV.   [101] Act I.   [102] Act IV.

keen, life-giving winds of science?"[103] Religion ought to be discussed on the stage, he said, if it "has any bearing upon character in England today"; if it is "effete and defunct ... the playwright can afford to treat it as a naturalist does an organ that has lapsed into a rudimentary stage."[104]

The clergymen in Jones's plays exhibit various attitudes. The scientists are nearly all agnostic. Professor Jopp of *Judah* does not say there is no God, but "Perhaps there is no great secret after all."[105] David Remon of *The Masqueraders* includes among the shadows, the phantoms of men "playing at religion." When Blanchflower remonstrates,

Oh, but surely, surely there is Something real Somewhere.... we must believe that there is—hum? eh?—a Kind of—eh?—a Sort of a Something—Somewhere, eh?

David answers, "If you like to believe that there is a kind of a sort of a something—somewhere—and you find it consoling, I'm as willing to pretend to believe that as anything else."[106] Later he says playfully:

My conjecture is that bad folks when they die are sent to Saturn to study current theology, and if at the end of five hundred years they know anything about it, their probation is complete.[107]

Dr. Carey in *The Physician* expresses agnosticism in stating a preference for hell:

Good common-sense citizens when they die—well, they think they go to heaven or hell, but they only go to limbo—and I should like to go to heaven *or* hell; the latter for preference, I think, because it's only when we suffer... we can make sure that we're alive.[108]

As Sir Stephen of *The Goal* dies he thinks of his dead wife, Peggie. "My Peggie! ... I shall see her again, I suppose—if it isn't all moonshine! ... I wonder if it is all moonshine!"[109] *The*

---

[103] "Religion on the Stage," *Nineteenth Century Review,* in *Renascence of the English Drama, op. cit.,* p. 35.
[104] *Ibid.,* p. 38.   [105] Act III.   [106] Act II.   [107] Act II.
[108] Act I.   [109] *Op. cit.,* p. 309.

Galilean's Victory offers an elaborate discussion of religion. In it the physiologist Richard Fyson and the chemist Philip Nuneham are agnostic. Fyson is described in the stage directions as "sceptical, cynical." He considers religion an excellent opiate for the people: ". . . if religion keeps working men from getting drunk and beating their wives, then religion must be an excellent thing for working men." His daughter Christabel may have religion "in whatever quantity or quality" she desires, but he cannot accept any religious doctrine for himself. He says:

. . . we have no working, workable, work-a-day religion in England, and therefore all our moral values are wrong and confused. Christianity is a horrible misfit for our modern civilisation. . . . I'm talking about religion as if it were a serious matter! Do, pray, forgive me!

Weak people, he says, look to religion to save themselves from the consequences of their behavior. On the other hand, he shakes hands with the evangelist Rebbings and says, "You're the man for my money!" because Rebbings believes in social and economic application of Christian ethics.[110] Finally, because science is honest, Fyson says: "Science is the only religion—."[111] Philip Nuneham agrees that:

We don't want a religion, at least we don't want a creed—the day for creeds and dogmas is over. Science and Truth must be our guides in the future. . . . It is to Science that we must look for the evolution of our new religion.[112]

Faced with the break-up of his home, Philip still refuses religion. He and Fyson conclude:

NUNE. . . . What we have to suffer, we'll suffer—we won't take spiritual drugs, eh?
. . . .
FYSON. No! We won't hocus-pocus ourselves. . . . But the masses will always need a panacea. And women—women will never be able to do without religion.[113]

[110] Act I.   [111] Act IV.   [112] Act I.   [113] Act IV.

Jones seems to agree with his scientists that religious dogma will not suffice as a guide for complex, thoughtful people. But he does not agree with some of his scientists that a morality drawn from nature is a proper guide. Addressing "Mrs. Grundy" in the Preface to *The Case of Rebellious Susan* (1894), Jones said: "Nature's morality is not your morality, nor mine. Nature has ten thousand various morals, all of them as shocking as truth itself."[114] I emphasize "nor mine." Jones's scientists who trust nature as a guide to conduct do not always speak for Jones. For example, Dulcie in *The Masqueraders*, under the spell of David Remon and his reasoning, debates the morality of marriage:

How if it isn't moral? Suppose it's horribly, horribly immoral! Moral! Moral!! Moral!!! Is there anything under God's sun so immoral, ah—guess it—guess it—to be married to a man one hates! And you go on plastering it and poulticing it and sugaring it over with "moral" and "ideal" and "respectable," and all those words that men use to cheat themselves with.[115]

David believes that the marriage-vow is man-made and that, without love, it has no value. When he wins Dulcie at cards, he dares Sir Brice to claim her: "Dare . . . to show your face in the home that my love shall give to her—and whatever laws men have made to bind you and her together, I'll break them and rid her of you!"[116] David rests his case on reason and on love. That may be a law of nature. But Jones believes in another law of nature, one that he calls "instinct." His spokesman is Helen, who says:

I can't reason at all. I can only feel, and I know my instinct is right. I know the woman who gives herself to another man while her husband is alive betrays her sex, and is a bad woman.[117]

"Nature's a sad bungler," says Dr. Carey in *The Physician*, and Jones sems to agree, for nature is "terribly careless and terribly cruel."[118] On the other hand, Jones speaks through his

---

[114] (London and New York, 1899), p. x.

[115] Act III.   [116] Act III.   [117] Act IV.   [118] Act II.

scientists whenever they invoke the laws of nature to support the points of view Jones feels as if by instinct to be right. Andrew Cutler in *The Divine Gift* (1912) is clearly Jones's spokesman: he is called a "sage" by the characters in the play, whose problems he solves. Cutler is a conservative; his conservatism is based upon the laws of nature. He speaks of woman suffrage and labor unrest as a "twin revolt against the detestable and tyrannical conditions which misguided Nature has . . . imposed upon the human species."[119] The adjective "misguided" applied to "Nature" is ironic, as the context indicates. Cutler addresses an ironic prayer to nature, to change the order of the universe, so that the "feeble, the diseased, and the worthless" might have more pleasant lives. Jones seems to feel that natural law offers invincible support, wherever it supports his "instincts."[120]

The foregoing data outline Jones's use of the principles of heredity in the creation of character, his concepts of men of science, and his use of ideas drawn from science.

The significance of the data goes deeper than a catalog of qualities. Dickinson pointed out that when Jones "builds a play around a character, that character is an embodied point of view,

---

[119] In Hamilton, ed., *op. cit.*, IV, Act I.

[120] In the portraits of extremists, Jones satirized other readings of natural law. Jones presented advanced thinkers, especially among his men of science, but as Marjorie Northend phrases it, "the 'advanced' thinkers who upset his theories of life and his respect for British tradition" are caricatures. ("Henry Arthur Jones and the Development of the Modern English Drama," *The Review of English Studies*, XVIII (January, 1942), 458.) The satire is especially evident in *Judah*. Jones seems to agree with the scientist Jopp, but Jopp's daughter Sophie carries the rationalism of science too far. She is a "dogmatic, supercilious, incisive young lady, with eye-glass and short hair. She speaks in a metallic, confident voice; a girl who could never blush." (Act I.) When Juxon proposes marriage to her, she raises physiological questions. Juxon, her male counterpart, thinks she is quite right and goes into an explanation of his physical condition, including an offer to bring her a certificate from the Insurance Society. In *The Crusaders* (1891) Burge Jawle, "the Great Pessimist Philosopher," bases his solemn pronouncements upon science. "Analyse your personal attractions," he says to the beautiful Cynthia. "Take a microscope. Look at your hand. . . . What is it? A coarse, scaly epidermis, studded with huge bristles—." (New York, 1893, Act II.) These people are scientific prigs, representing, I think, Jones's tendency to accept science just so far, but to draw back from the full implications of scientific rationalism.

a crux in the social fabric."[121] When Jones built plays around Judah Llewellyn and Professor Jopp, David Remon, Michael, Dr. Carey, the scientists and clergymen of *The Galilean's Victory*, and Andrew Cutler of *The Divine Gift*, he was trying to say something, to express views that would clash with one another and provoke his audience to thought. He attributed to his scientists extreme views with which he did not always agree. Through other characters and through the outcome of the action, he stated his own conservative views. He sought to be just, to present problems as problems, but he would not end a play with the tentative, problem-play ending of the Ibsen school. It was his practice to provide a conservative answer, usually tacked on in the last act after the point at which an Ibsen would have closed the play.

In *Judah*, for instance, Jones is intellectually on the side of Jopp, against miracle-working and charlatanism. But he is emotionally on the side of Judah and Vashti. His solution is to let Jopp win a complete victory and then concede it. The out-and-out charlatan Dethic is denounced and sent away; but when Judah and Vashti are given the courage to acknowledge their lie, Jopp pledges them his friendship. Emotionally, the victory belongs to Judah.

The case is clearer in *The Masqueraders*. Toward marriage David Remon stands for the rational view encouraged by science, that a woman should be free to break a marriage tie already broken and even degraded by the insulting, lecherous, and brutal conduct of her husband. Jones states the case with utmost fairness. Sir Brice buys Dulcie with his money as a kind of defiance toward Lady Clarice; Dulcie submits to purchase, but intends to be a good wife. Afterward, Sir Brice neglects her, spends his time with the commonest girls of the music halls, quarrels with her, satirizes her in public, alienates her friends, employs physical violence, refers to her child as a brat, and

---

[121] Thomas H. Dickinson, *The Contemporary Drama of England* (Boston, 1920), pp. 93-94.

forces her to use David Remon's money to pay for his gambling and dissipation. When he forces her to admit that she loves David, he says:

SIR BRICE. . . . Go on loving him. You needn't hesitate. He expects a fair exchange—if he hasn't already got it.
DULCIE. . . . That's a lie, and you know it.
SIR BRICE. Very well. It's a lie. I don't care one way or the other. Get me some money.[122]

Finally Sir Brice gambles Dulcie and her child against David's entire fortune, on the turn of a card. Jones builds up a powerful, rational case against the horrible martyrdom, even the immorality, of adherence to the letter of the marriage vow between Dulcie and Sir Brice. Remon's philosophy supports this case completely: "My wife! My child! Come! You're mine!"[123] he says in all candor. The play might have ended there, a kind of Ibsen-drama sternly opposed to a false convention. But it is not Jones's case. His case is stated by Helen in the added fourth act. No matter what the circumstances, the marriage vow is sacred. Instinct demands it.

In *Michael and His Lost Angel,* Michael and Audrie discuss the philosophic basis upon which the action of the play rests. Though neither is a scientist, the law that operates is stated in scientific terms. Michael reaches out to Audrie in the hope of drawing her upward, but he is warned:

AUDRIE. Do you think that you can have any influence on my soul without my having an equal influence on yours?
MICHAEL. Action and reaction are equal and opposite. You think that law prevails in the spiritual world as well as in the material world?
AUDRIE. I'm sure it does.[124]

The law proves stronger than Michael's intention. It is worked out to its logical conclusion when Michael tells Audrie he is not sorry. If the curtain had come down then or when Michael had resigned the Church for Audrie as Judah did for Vashti, it

[122] Act III. [123] Act III. [124] Act I.

would have stated the case for science. But it is not Jones's case. He could not see Audrie divorced and Michael happy with her. Jones tugs her toward spirituality until she dies, apparently of exhaustion.

Dr. Carey of *The Physician* is more liberal in his ideas than Jones. He has a strong attachment for Lady Valerie and is willing to marry her, if she might be divorced. But Jones rejects this possibility and has Carey fall in love with an ingénue in white muslin, for whom he is willing to give up, at least temporarily, his researches in cholera—his life-work.

The scientists in *The Galilean's Victory* represent agnostic points of view personified, played against the views held by a variety of clergymen. The views of the clergymen are narrow, dogmatic, and institutional, except those of Rebbings the evangelist, whose application of Christian ethics wins the "Galilean's victory." Jones, trying to state these different views fairly, gets involved in contradictions. He seems to agree with his scientists, described as "strong-minded, fair-minded, entirely truthful and sincere," that religion is a delusion, hocus-pocus, but a useful drug to keep working-men at work and women at home. He seems to agree with Rebbings's application of Christian ethics. But apparently he does not suppose the same ethics should extend to Nuneham's treatment of Christabel, and apparently he does not even see that the use of an evangelist by a pair of agnostic scientists, to forestall a strike, is reprehensible if not consciously cynical.

Cutler in *The Divine Gift* is a sociologist, with enough natural science to call upon the laws of nature to support opposition to woman suffrage and the labor movement. He seems to represent accurately Jones's view of 1912. Jones no longer felt it necessary, as in *The Masqueraders*, to provide thoughtful content for a play by presenting views more radical than his own. The necessity for presenting a challenging point of view and building up a strong case for it, belongs, it would seem, to the period of transition from melodrama to drama.

To present challenging points of view fairly and even attractively, Jones had to ponder them and consider what might be said for them. In fact, he was for a while considered liberal; he was intimate with Shaw and William Morris. But he drew back from radical conclusions because of an ingrained conservatism; he opposed them through spokesmen who rested their case on instinct. The conflict in Jones's mind produced a good deal of confusion in his plays. He wanted his dramas to say something, but he did not always know what. His first ending for the melodrama *Saints and Sinners* was unhappy, challenging the convention of a happy ending. In stage production the ending was changed to a happy one. Concerning this change, Cordell remarks:

... this early patched-up ending set a bad precedent for Jones, who was rarely courageous (or, in his day, foolhardy?) enough to follow his conception of character and circumstances to their logical end. One easily forgets that he was a pioneer.[125]

Pioneering, Jones was often confused in acceptance or rejection of the implications of science. He presents Jopp as an honest, right-thinking man, a representative of the attitude of science, but presents Jopp's daughter, who represents the same attitude carried to its logical end, as ridiculous. Jones produced *The Crusaders* with hope and high endeavor, including settings and furniture designed by William Morris.[126] The play failed because it strikes out in all directions and means no one thing. He labored long and hard on *The Tempter,* but presented a Devil who is a confusing compound of tempter and puppet-master. I cannot tell what Jones meant in the last act of *The Masqueraders.* Three acts of the play say that a loveless marriage should be broken, and break it; the fourth act says at the climax that it should not be broken, but the dénouement both leaves Dulcie to her old husband and, with the symbol of David's mother's wedding ring, marries her to David, if he should come

---
[125] *Op. cit.,* p. 69.
[126] Doris Arthur Jones, *op. cit.,* p. 119.

back from Africa alive. This is no problem-ending; it is a blur. The ending of *The Physician* marries a middle-aged research-physician to a girl in a country town. The concluding statement that the choice lies between the girl or completion of Dr. Carey's research does not imply happiness. As Cordell points out of *The Galilean's Victory,* "the scientific rationalism of Fyson and Nuneham promptly desert them when Christabel confesses her infidelity."[127] Christabel's lover also deserts her, and the play ends in a statement of mid-Victorian prejudices and selected doctrines of Christian Socialism. The firmly handled ending of *The Knife* in 1909 was, says Cordell, "revolutionary for Jones."[128]

None the less, Jones's dramas did effectively support his crusade to reform the drama and bring it abreast of the other literature of the late Victorian age. He advanced from melodrama to drama by making thoughtful use of the principles of heredity in his creation of character, by presenting men of science as spokesmen for the ideas of science, and by attempting fair presentation of revolutionary views with which he did not agree. Because Jones, born in 1851, brought up by a Baptist deacon, self-educated through reading, and conservative in temperament, wished his plays to support what he believed to be truth, his plays fail to be firm, clear, and as radical as science.

But after all, Jones was a pioneer in a period of transition. A writer of successful melodramas briefly attracted to the Ibsen-drama, Jones turned for the substance of transition to his own reading of science. The mutation from *The Middleman* to *Judah* and *The Masqueraders* is largely due to his meditation of the science underlying them.

[127] *Op. cit.,* p. 187.
[128] *Ibid.,* p. 190.

JAMES OSLER BAILEY
The University of North Carolina

www.ingramcontent.com/pod-product-compliance
Lightning Source LLC
Chambersburg PA
CBHW030112010526
44116CB00005B/206